Who Says You Can't Buy a Home!

Who Says You Can't Buy a Home!

David Reed

₄AMACOM

American Management Association

New York • Atlanta • Brussels • Chicago • Mexico City • San Francisco
Shanghai • Tokyo • Toronto • Washington, D.C.

This publication is designed to provide accurate and authoritative
information in regard to the subject matter covered. It is sold with the
understanding that the publisher is not engaged in rendering legal,
accounting, or other professional service. If legal advice or other expert
assistance is required, the services of a competent professional person
should be sought.

Library of Congress Cataloging-in-Publication Data

Reed, David (Carl David), 1957–
    Who says you can't buy a home! : how to put credit problems, down payment
challenges, and income issues behind you— and get a mortgage now / David Reed.
        p.   cm.
    Includes index.
    ISBN-10: 0-8144-7340-7
    ISBN-13: 978-08144-7340-5
    1. Mortgage loans—United States.   2. House buying—United
States.   I. Title.

HG2040.5.U5R43   2006
332.7′220973—dc22

2006002459

Printing number

10   9   8   7   6   5   4   3   2   1

This book is dedicated to my wife Cindy, whom I adore.

Contents

Who Says You Can't Buy a Home!

Introduction

If you picked up this book, you most likely have some unique requirements. Buying a home without money for a down payment, whether you have good credit, bad credit, or no credit, is common today. In fact, it's been a reality for quite some time in the lending business. Do you have no income or no job? Do you have difficulty documenting your income, or is your income not considered "qualified"? Well, you'll still need to be able to make the mortgage payment, but there are mortgage programs that don't verify any income.

Bankruptcy? No problem. Foreclosure? No problem. A brand new job and the lender won't count your income? No problem. No cash? Again, no problem.

There are no tricks or gadgets in this book. You won't have to send us any money for a three-week course or attend a seminar at some hotel somewhere. And an added bonus is that you don't have to sit through a two-hour infomercial on your local cable television station. Everything you read has been proven in today's market and is being used every day by people just like yourself.

The problem is that most of these strategies simply aren't advertised or marketed properly. This book will shed new light on how people actually buy a home without a down payment, even with credit or income issues—all the while using "off the shelf" programs.

Face it, lenders make money by making loans. That's why they're called "lenders," right? Some lenders choose to make home loans to everyday borrowers, those with a monthly paycheck, 20 percent down, and excellent credit. Other lenders like to make loans to qualified veterans. Or they're FHA lenders who make money by issuing HUD loans.

But nearly one out of five loans don't fall into these categories. Some lenders (actually lots of them) make loans to people who don't quite fit the "mold" from a credit standpoint. These lenders, sometimes called "subprime" lenders because their loans go to people whose credit is "less than prime," understand that sometimes bad things happen to good people, and they're willing to help them out. Still other loans are designed for those who have income that is considered "hard to prove" from an underwriter's perspective. The income may be there, but for any of a number of reasons, that income can't be used for loan qualifying.

I've been in the mortgage business for nearly 20 years, and I've placed people in homes under almost every circumstance imaginable. I began my career in mortgage lending as a mortgage broker in San Diego, California, and I learned home loans through the School of Hard Knocks. As a broker, I was able to compare literally every major lender in the country. Each time a new loan program was introduced, I would study it carefully, then find a market that could use that new product.

A few years later, as a mortgage banker in Texas, I got heavily involved in the subprime mortgage business. It was here that I learned the ins and outs of how mortgages can be made to people with damaged credit. These loans are a different breed, and they aren't approved in the same way a conventional or VA loan would be. Then I was a vice president in the Internet mortgage division of one of the largest banks in the South, placing almost every sort of home loan available from Miami to Arlington to Dallas.

I've seen it all, and I've issued almost every type of loan available in today's marketplace. Most likely, I've placed people whose credit is 10 times worse than yours into homes. Perhaps most important, I am a mortgage banker. A real loan officer. Most home-buying books that you find are written by people who have never placed a mortgage loan in their life. This book is based on real life, not on lending "theories," but on actual programs that you can use today.

If you want to own your own home but don't think you can qualify, this is your book. Congratulations; you're on your way to homeownership!

Where to Find Mortgages

Mortgage loans come from four basic sources: retail banks, savings and loan institutions or credit unions, and mortgage bankers or mortgage brokers. They can also come from individuals who invest in mortgage loans and real estate by providing people with the money to buy houses.

Retail banks are certainly the most common source. They're everywhere, right? Banks want your checking account, your money market account, your credit cards, and your mortgage. They also want your car loan, your student loan, your life insurance, and your investments. Banks want everything you have, financially speaking.

Savings and loan institutions and credit unions are another source of mortgage money. They operate much like banks in that they also perform some of the other financial functions that a bank does. A bank, a savings and loan, and a credit union all offer deposit services, automobile loans, and a host of other financial products as part of their overall business strategy.

The next group of mortgage lenders doesn't have a building on every street corner, but they're certainly as common: mortgage bankers.

Mortgage bankers do one thing—make mortgages. They don't offer savings accounts or make automobile loans or any other type of consumer loan. They make mortgages, using money that they borrow.

Yep, just as you and I can borrow money to buy a house, mortgage

3

bankers can also borrow money to lend to us. But mortgage bankers borrow bigger chunks and have a history of borrowing money and paying it back regularly. Where you or I might borrow $200,000 to buy a house, a mortgage banker may have a credit line of, say, $500 million.

Mortgage brokers make at least half of all the mortgages produced in the United States. In some areas their market share is greater, and in other areas it's not as great. But they have become a huge influence in the mortgage market since the late 1980s.

Unlike mortgage bankers, mortgage brokers do not lend their own money. Instead, they find money for other people. They can probably be most accurately compared to independent insurance agents. An independent insurance agent doesn't work for just one insurance company, but has access to a whole list of insurance companies.

Mortgage brokers find their loans on a "wholesale" basis, meaning that they get access to mortgage loans at prices well below retail, so getting a loan through them is not more expensive than getting a mortgage directly from the lender. (At least, using a mortgage broker shouldn't be more expensive; a broker determines its own charges.) Mortgage brokers attempt to find the best program for their client, mark that loan up to "retail," and keep the difference, or the spread.

Mortgage brokers have access to hundreds of wholesale lenders. These wholesale lenders find mortgage brokers and enroll those brokers to market their mortgage products for them.

Mortgage companies use brokers because it's cheaper for them. It's expensive to find a building, hire a staff, pay taxes, and insure the whole operation. A mortgage broker can open up a shop, contact a few wholesale operators, and get the wholesalers' business right away.

Because brokers don't issue loan approvals or print closing papers, they have very little control over the process once the loan package has been submitted to the lender for underwriting. That's a big disadvantage of using a broker: The broker loses control of your file.

If a lender is really, really busy and your loan is 159th in the loan stack, there's very little a broker can do to move you up in the line so that your loan is approved more quickly. If an underwriter has a question about your file, he doesn't ask you; instead, he asks the loan processor who works with the loan officer at the mortgage broker's office. The loan processor asks the loan officer, who eventually will ask you something like, "You said you just graduated from college last fall; do you have a transcript proving that you were in school? We need to establish a two-year employment history" or some other underwriting question.

After that question is answered, your information goes back up the food chain to the underwriter, who then moves forward. Your file goes to a closing department and maybe to some attorneys for review; your papers are then drawn up and delivered to the closing agent. That's a lot of people and things to do. That's why good customer service from a lender to a broker is paramount.

Mortgage bankers, on the other hand, have more control, because it's the banker that takes the loan from origination to final funding. Things can move more quickly with a banker because there's no "hand-off" from your broker to a lender. It's all done in one house.

A mortgage banker may also be more recognizable to you. It may be a national name that you see on television or that advertises in your local newspaper. A mortgage banker may also be a division of your bank. If you have a checking account or a bank credit card, it's likely that your bank also has a mortgage banking operation. When you get a mortgage there, you're dealing with someone you know and trust. You're familiar with the company.

Mortgage bankers will generally have rates similar to those of mortgage brokers; however, a large mortgage banker might "price in" its recognizable status: "Yeah, our rate may be slightly higher, but hey, we're your bank." To many people, having a slightly higher rate is worth it when the alternative is finding a mortgage broker and getting rate quotes from people they've never heard of.

There are a couple of other options related to the broker versus banker question that are essentially different variations on the mortgage marketing theme: net branches and correspondent lenders.

Both are types of mortgage bankers; they approve the loan and provide final funding for it. You're dealing with the same loan company from start to finish. A net branch is an operation that is wholly owned by a mortgage banking company, but the people who manage and run the branch are independent. The owner of a net branch will get all its mortgages through the mortgage banking company, but will run the mortgage operation as if it were an independent broker.

The net branch will pay the rent, employee salaries, advertising, and just about any business expense needed to run the operation. The benefit of a net branch is that it's run by mortgage bankers, who exercise more control of the loan process than a broker does. A net branch will find a loan, send it to underwriting, get approval, and fund the loan with the mortgage banker's credit line. The net branch will get a below-market interest rate, just like a broker, then mark up the rate to whatever it wants and keep the difference.

A similar, yet more established, arrangement is a mortgage banking company that uses correspondent lenders. This type of mortgage banking firm is typically much smaller than most mortgage bankers and is usually regional or focusing on one city. Such a company also operates just like a banker, but unlike a net branch operation, it is also able to "shop" the mortgage application around for the best rate or to locate a hard-to-find loan program.

An independent mortgage banker that works with correspondent lenders just might be the best choice for finding a lender. Such a banker has the same control over the loan process as traditional bankers do, yet it is able to shop the mortgage around for the best price and terms just as a broker does.

These mortgage bankers will rarely service your loan; instead, they will have arranged ahead of time who your lender will be. Your first payment will usually be to the correspondent lender they've agreed to sell the loan to. Almost every national mortgage banking company you've ever heard of also operates correspondent lending divisions.

Another new source of mortgages is really a new method of securing a mortgage rather than being different from traditional mortgage options—online lenders. Online companies have finally become more mainstream. In fact, almost every "bricks-and-mortar" lender also has a method of applying online. E-Loan, for example, started in 1997 as one of the first true "online" lenders. E-Loan actually started out as a mortgage broker but eventually became a mortgage banker as well. Soon, other online ventures began to appear and to be heavily marketed. Such marketing soon allowed such names as E-Loan and DiTech to become household names in the mortgage industry.

Another online mortgage model was established and is practiced by Lending Tree. Lending Tree is not a lender itself; instead, it allows you to fill out an online loan application so that other lenders can "bid" on your loan. After you complete your loan application with Lending Tree, these other lenders review your loan and can make you an offer. You then choose which loan looks best to you.

So with all these choices, who do you choose? Unless you're completely comfortable with the mortgage process and this isn't the first time you've gotten a home loan, I suggest staying away from online companies. When it comes time to answer questions and hold hands, someone on the other end of a telephone simply can't match the customer service that an experienced face-to-face loan officer can. But there is no clear-cut choice as to which is better. The clear-cut answer? Apply at both a broker and a banker and have them compete for your loan.

Mortgages from Individuals

Home loans can also be made by individuals as well as by banks, bankers, or brokers. Financing private real estate is a big business. A private investor might buy a house, turn it into a rental, and collect monthly payments. If an investor pays $100,000 for a house and gets a 6.00 percent 30-year fixed-rate mortgage, then the monthly payments would be about $600 per month. If she charges $1,000 a month, then there's a monthly profit of $400. No big secret there.

Other investors might buy a house, fix it up, and then resell the house for a profit. Still other real estate investors act like a private bank and make loans directly to individuals to help them buy a home.

If the rates and terms offered by an individual are competitive and you're not being beaten up by a loan officer or mortgage company underwriter by paperwork, then there's a strong case to be made for using a private party.

Typically however, private financing becomes an option when the applicant doesn't qualify for a conventional loan from a banker or broker. And private investors know this. If you have gone through a few lenders and you have not been approved for a loan, then there are at least one or two problems with your application. Either your credit isn't up to par or your income is difficult to prove. Mortgage lenders make loans in accordance with previously established guidelines, and even though exceptions are made every day in the mortgage market, they're also few—that's why they're called exceptions.

Private investors usually charge higher interest rates than a banker or broker does. Why? Well, because they can. If a lender has turned someone down for some particular reason, that means there's an increased level of risk. Lenders, including individual ones, attempt to offset that risk by charging more for their money.

Individuals who use private investors have typically exhausted their other resources before turning to an individual real estate investor. I'll give you an example. Several years ago, my in-laws decided that they wanted to move to another state. They bought their new home and put the old one up on the market. Several weeks went by, but hardly anyone came by to look at their property. There wasn't anything wrong with the house or anything necessarily wrong with the location, but few people took the time to look at it. After a couple of months, they were contacted by someone who was interested in buying the house. They showed him the house, and he determined that, yes, that was the house for him. So he made an offer. There was one problem, though: He couldn't get approved by a lender, and he didn't have enough money to pay cash. Dead deal, right? Wrong.

My father-in-law asked to see a copy of the buyer's credit report, which he quickly showed them. He did not have bad credit; in fact, he had good credit. There were no bankruptcies or collection accounts of any sort. But he had been turned down by three different lenders. Why? He had opened an automobile repair shop less then six months ago, and no bank would touch him until he had been in business, successfully, for at least two years. So he was stuck.

But, the buyer suggested, he did have some down payment money.

He could give 10 percent down right away if my in-laws would carry a note for him. At the time, interest rates were around 7.00 percent. My in-laws made a counteroffer: Yes, we'll carry the note for you, but in addition to 10 percent down, we'll charge 8.00 percent instead of market rates, and after five years we'll ask that you refinance the note somewhere else or otherwise retire the loan.

The buyer agreed. As a matter of fact, he refinanced the note after two years, paying off my in-laws three years early. (That didn't quite set that well with them at the time—after all, they were making a steady 8.00 percent return on their funds at a time when other investments were losing money hand over fist!)

People don't seek out private investors only because they have terrible credit, although that's often the case. Nor do they need private financing because all their income is derived from drug sales or sticking up grocery stores. No, most private financing is simply the result of not qualifying under conventional lending guidelines because for some reason the buyer's income can't be used, or because she hasn't been at a job long enough or has recently started her own business.

CHAPTER 2

The Key People in Your Approval Process

$\mathbf{W}$ho are these key people, anyway? Whatever part of the country you're in, you'll find job titles seen in no place other than real estate financing. Did you know there was such a thing as an escrow officer? Did you know there are abstract attorneys looking, well, at abstracts? What about surveyors? Appraisers? Flood reporters? Title insurers? Goodness. What a mess of people.

But knowing who the key people in the transaction are will give you a leg up in terms of knowing how the process works and who does what, when, and where.

Key People

The Loan Officer

This is your key contact. If you've played your cards right, you met this person long before you went shopping for a home. The loan officer can be a representative of a bank or a mortgage company and has several key jobs.

The first job is to acquire the loan business. He does that by establishing a market base. Most often this market base is a collection of real estate offices or home builders, but it doesn't have to be. Loan officers can get business anywhere they want, as long, of course, as they get enough to keep them in business.

Some loan officers get their business from accounting firms or legal firms. Others advertise in newspapers or magazines or put on seminars for the general public. Also, after a few years in the business, the loan officer will have built up his own database of previous clients.

Your loan officer is the person who shepherds you through the loan process. She will take your application, run your credit report, and prequalify you based upon your debt ratios and credit grading. Loans are available for almost any credit grade, and it's the loan officer's responsibility to make sure that you get the best loan possible given your particular circumstances.

The loan officer will show you available mortgage programs that you can qualify for. If you have zero available for a down payment, you'll get zero-down choices. If you want a fixed rate with 20 percent down, you'll have those choices. If there are problems with the loan during the process, it's your loan officer who helps correct any problems and gets you back on track.

The loan officer will also provide you with your "Good Faith Estimate of Settlement Charges," often just called the Good Faith. The Good Faith is the list of fees you can expect during the loan process in addition to your down payment, should you make one. The loan officer will also provide you with various state and federal disclosures about mortgage loans for you to review and sign. Sometimes you'll get these disclosures when you make your loan application and sometimes you'll get them in the mail.

If you apply online, you'll be assigned a loan officer who will perform the same functions. Most online applications will allow you to indicate the type of loan you're looking for or to simply say, "Tell me what loans I can get." With either method, online or face to face, your loan officer is your key contact.

The Loan Processor

After you turn in your application and select the type of loan you want, your application will be handed over to the person who will help document your file, the loan processor.

Documentation means that the processor will take personal information and documents from you, such as your paycheck stubs and W2s to verify your income, and items such as bank statements to verify your assets, insurance information to get homeowner's coverage, and anything else that the lender needs in order to approve your loan.

At this stage, the loan processor is working on your loan file every day, whereas your loan officer is out getting other loans. Your primary contact will now be the loan processor, and this will continue to be true through the closing of your loan—that is, unless there are problems and your loan officer needs to get involved.

Your loan processor also gathers other documentation that you won't be able to provide, such as the appraisal of the property, the title report, and any legal work that might need to be done. The loan processor makes sure that the loan is in fact ready to be submitted to the underwriter for approval.

The Underwriter

The underwriter is the person who reviews the loan submitted by the loan processor and ensures that it meets lending guidelines. If a particular loan requires $10,000 down, then the underwriter will look for proof that you have $10,000 available by reviewing the bank statements that you provided. Or perhaps the loan program requires that your total monthly bills represent less than 40 percent of your gross monthly income.

Whatever the loan requires, it's the underwriter who has the final say. The underwriter might also issue *loan conditions*. A loan is generally approved as long as certain conditions are met. Such a condition might be one more recent pay stub, or maybe the loan processor will have to verbally verify your employment by calling your boss or your company's human resources department. Loan conditions are discussed in more detail later in the chapter.

There may be other information that the underwriter needs. Perhaps the underwriter has questions about the appraisal that need to be answered. For instance, one of the houses used in your appraisal may have been much farther away from the house you're buying than is normal. The underwriter might ask for information on another recent home sale in your neighborhood as a loan condition. If so, your loan officer or processor will call the appraiser and ask for the additional information.

After you or your loan officer meets your loan conditions and the underwriter approves the results, your loan then goes to the Document Department.

The Document Department

This department goes over your approval one final time, making sure that whatever the underwriter asked for is in the file, and at the same time making sure that the loan papers that are about to be printed both are legal and meet the requirements of the loan you're applying for.

This department will also deliver your closing papers, either electronically or by using a courier, to whoever is handling your closing.

The Closer

Depending upon where you live, the person handling the closing might be an attorney, a title representative, or an escrow officer. Whoever it is, this person's job is to make sure that you sign where you're supposed to sign and that you are who you say you are.

Your signatures are witnessed and notarized, and all legal documentation is gathered and returned to the lender. When you have signed all the papers, at the end of the day your loan is completed. Congratulations.

Other Important People in the Transaction

There are also other people outside of the mortgage company that you need to be familiar with. These people are the inspector, the appraiser, the attorney, and the surveyor. In some states, certain responsibilities may be handled by different people or one person may provide more than one function, but the overall requirements vary little from state to state.

The Inspector

This person makes a physical evaluation of the home you want to buy. In some areas, this person may also determine whether there are termites or other wood-destroying pests in your prospective home. It's the inspector who looks for things like light switches that don't work, doors that don't close, roofs that leak, or faulty furnaces.

It's not just the lender that wants to make sure the house is in good shape. You'll want to know if there are problems with the house that you'll need to take care of once you own it. Typically, the seller of a home is required to disclose everything that she knows is wrong with the home. But an inspector will take a fine-toothed comb and go over the house for any defects. He will even flush the toilets and make sure the garbage disposal works.

The Appraiser

The appraiser helps to determine the market value of your home, and is not to be confused with the inspector. When a lender makes a loan, it bases its judgment not just on you, but on the collateral (the home) as well. If the home is not worth the price you paid for it, you will have trouble getting the loan.

The appraiser will compare your home to other homes in the area that have recently been sold to make sure the price is in the right range. She will also look at whether your house is unusual or markedly different from others in your neighborhood. Lenders like to see "comparable sales," or sales of other homes that are comparable to yours. If your property is very unusual, they worry about whether they can sell it quickly should they have to foreclose.

The Surveyor

This person makes certain that your property lines are correctly identified, that your house is sitting where it's supposed to be, and that there are no encroachments, or other private property that crosses your property lines. An encroachment could be a trail, fence, or road that crosses your property line.

The survey is usually a drawing showing the exact location of the property lines and where your house sits upon that property. Sometimes a neighbor's fence wanders onto your property or there's a long-used road or trail that crosses the property.

The Title Agent

The title agent will generate a report giving the history of who has owned your property. This will go back to who owned the land when your house was built, and will indicate who sold it to whom over the years.

The title report will also note any easements that the property might have. An *easement* is access to your property by someone else. The electric company might have an easement, or a right of access, to your property to get to its utility pole. Or the cable company might show that it has access rights to your property to lay a cable line.

The title agent will make sure that the property changes hands in a legal manner and that all previous claims to your property have been settled. Who performs this function will vary depending upon where you live; sometimes it's a real estate attorney, and sometimes it's a closer.

Automated Underwriting Systems

Some loans are still processed the old-fashioned way, but most lenders have developed automated underwriting systems, or AUSs, that take various parts of the loan profile and come up with an approval. With an AUS, loan approvals are issued at the very beginning of the loan process, not at the end. Your loan still has to go to the loan officer, the loan processor, the underwriter, and the closer, but you need to provide the lender with only exactly what is required to close the loan instead of providing everything imaginable that might possibly be asked for beforehand.

Just a few short years ago, it would take a few weeks just to get the loan to a loan underwriter. This was through no fault of the borrower.

There are so many people involved in the exchange of real estate that it simply takes time to get everything together and to put everything in the order it needs to be in. But now we've turned things around.

An AUS takes the borrower's information and the sales price of the home and makes a loan determination. The AUS will run a bunch of numbers, pull some credit reports, evaluate your assets, and look at some credit scores, then automatically spit out a loan approval. This process helps both the borrower and the lender because now the lender needs only exactly what the AUS approval asks for.

In the past, documentation would be provided just in case the underwriter wanted to review it. Now, however, documentation may not be needed unless the AUS asks for it. I'll give you an example. A few years ago, a borrower would sit in front of a loan officer and provide the following:

Completed loan application and authorization forms

Two most recent pay stubs

Two most recent W2 forms

Three most recent bank statements

Three most recent investment statements

Copy of a divorce decree, if the borrower had been divorced

Two years most recent tax returns, all schedules

Explanation letters for any derogatory credit information that appeared

Names and phone number of all employers over the previous two years

Names and addresses of previous landlords

Copy of 12 months rent checks if renting

Now the applicant needs to provide documentation only for things the AUS asks for. No more and no less. Lenders want to streamline the approval process just as much as you do, and AUSs help to do just that. People with sterling credit and a stable income source will be asked for less documentation. Those whose income is perhaps more difficult to prove, those with credit concerns, those with little or no down payment, or those with any combination of those three issues will be asked to provide a little more information. It's sometimes a moving target, but the trick is to apply first, then supply only what's asked for. Nothing more and nothing less.

Who uses these new systems? Every lender uses them in one fashion or another. Practically every conventional and government loan gets an online approval using an AUS. And not just loans for those with decent credit.

Subprime lenders—those who specialize in issuing mortgages to people with damaged credit—also can use automated underwriting systems. They may not use the same ones that were developed for conventional underwriting, but they use some type of system that pulls a credit report and a credit score, evaluates debt ratios, and also looks at down payment requirements (if any) and any other factors that might affect mortgage approval.

AUSs are a big reason why loans can close in a matter of days and not weeks, especially for those with excellent credit histories. People who have great credit and high credit scores typically require much less documentation than those with average or marginal credit.

Another advantage of an AUS is that it gives the loan officer the ability to "tweak" your approval. Tweaking means changing certain aspects of your application to obtain approval.

For instance, suppose your loan officer submits your loan for an automated approval. The loan amount is $200,000, and your rate is 5.25 percent on a 15-year fixed rate. Then "uh-oh"—the system doesn't issue an approval. So your loan officer tries a 30-year fixed rate at 5.75 percent on the exact same loan amount, and you get your approval.

Prior to an AUS, there was no such thing as tweaking. A loan would have to be submitted to an underwriter with the 15-year fixed rate, and if it was declined, it would be returned to the loan officer, who would then rework the file, probably using the 30-year fixed-rate loan program.

You can also tweak your income by trying to get a raise at work. Or you can tweak your loan program from a 30-year fixed rate to a 3/1 hybrid that has a lower rate. You can literally play "what if" scenarios as long as you can stand it. But however you get your approval after tweaking, it's a lot more fun shopping for a home when you've got your approval in your hands.

But hold your horses; don't move in just yet. Your loan is likely to be only conditionally approved.

Loan conditions are part of loan life. Every loan I've ever closed, and I've closed a bunch of them, had loan conditions. What are they? Conditions are certain things that must happen or be provided before a mortgage loan will actually be approved, funded, and recorded. It's actually a level of approval, much like prequalification and preapprovals. Loan conditions are put in place instead of simply declining or setting aside a loan application. An underwriter will typically place loan conditions on an approval prior to issuing final mortgage funds. Common loan conditions are things such as one more recent pay stub if the ones in the file are more than 30 days old. In this case, the underwriter isn't going to turn down the loan application simply because the pay stubs are older than required. Instead, the underwriter will assume that the borrower still has his job, but one more stub will need to be provided. There are "prior to document" conditions and "prior to funding" conditions.

Prior to document conditions are things that need to be addressed before loan papers will be printed. That means that the underwriter isn't flat-out declining the loan, but there are certain questions that need to be answered before the loan can move forward. For instance, a couple claimed rental income on a property they owned. The loan officer put the rental income on the application, and the underwriter used it to determine debt ratios, but there was no evidence of the rental income in the file. No rent checks or income tax returns showing rental income were provided at the time of the initial loan application.

The borrowers were asked to provide some sort of documentation that could prove that they had the rental income they needed to qualify for the loan. The borrowers then supplied tax returns showing a history of rental income. The underwriter signed off on the condition and sent the loan to closing for loan documents to be printed.

Those same borrowers also had prior to funding conditions. These conditions, called PTCs, are less serious things that need to be addressed. The underwriter is willing to print closing papers, but before money actually changes hands, the underwriter wants to make certain that the PTCs are fulfilled. A common PTC would be evidence of sufficient hazard insurance to cover the property or that the title report needed to reflect the correct names of the new owners.

All loans come with conditions. You just need to know which ones matter most and when. You also need to be careful about some conditions. Sometimes answering one question gives rise to several others. In the case of the same couple that had rental income, the underwriter asked for rent verification. Their loan officer told them to get copies of their old tax returns and send them in. The borrowers did just that, thinking that everything was moving along. Wrong.

While the income tax returns did in fact show rental income, they also showed a substantial business loss for a home-based business that one of the borrowers ran. The business, a catering company, was a small affair that provided food and drinks for local functions. The borrowers weren't making any money on the business, so they didn't include it on their loan application.

The problem was not that they weren't making any money; the problem was that they deducted a significant amount of business expenses, leading to their taking a loss. This loss had to be subtracted from the income they put on their application.

Suddenly, there was a new condition spawned by a previous one. The underwriter wanted to see a year-to-date profit and loss statement prepared by their accountant before the loan could move forward. The borrowers didn't have an accountant, so they provided a statement that they made up themselves, showing not a loss, but a profit.

The problem with self-generated profit and loss (P&L) statements is that there are no quality-control checks. In other words, there's nothing to show that the borrowers have not lied on their P&L just to qualify for the loan. That's why underwriters typically won't accept self-generated P&Ls as proof of bona fide income. The couple was stuck, about to lose their home.

The underwriter then asked for 12 months' business bank statements. This the borrowers had. They provided the underwriter with 12 months' bank statements from their catering business that in fact matched up with the P&L they provided. This was good enough for the underwriter. The loan went to closing and was funded the next day.

CHAPTER 3

Types of Mortgage Loans

Mortgages come in all shapes and sizes. You can see the ads on television or read about them in the newspaper: "We have over 500 loans programs from which to choose!" I can recall working for a mortgage company that had rate sheets for its consumers that were eight pages long with over 125 different loan programs. Why all the loans?

There really aren't that many types of loans at all. It's just that lenders like to make it appear that they are giving you more "choices" than the other lender. But in reality, loans come in two types: fixed rate and adjustable rate.

Fixed Rates

Fixed rates are easy to explain. You get an interest rate when you take out your mortgage, and it's fixed. It doesn't change. Ever. Easy enough, right? The only thing you need to decide about your fixed rate is what the rate will be and over what period you'd like to amortize the loan. The amortization period is the fixed period over which your loan will be paid back. If your amortization period is 20 years, then your loan will be paid off exactly in 20 years and your monthly payments will remain the same, fixed, throughout the life of the mortgage.

Amortization periods can be anything the lender is willing to offer, but if a lender wants the loan to conform to Fannie Mae or Freddie Mac standards (discussed later in the book), then it will be amortized over 10, 15, 20, 25, 30, or sometimes 40 years. The differences between these loans are the rate and how much interest you will pay over the life of the loan. The longer the loan term, the lower your payment, simply because you're taking a longer period to pay back the lender.

For example, on a $100,000 15-year fixed-rate mortgage, you might get a rate of 5.00 percent. That means that your payments will be $790 per month. After 15 years, you will have paid the lender a total of $142,342. That means that the lender made $42,342 in interest charges.

Borrowing the same amount for 30 years at 5.50 percent works out to a monthly amount of $567. Over 30 years, that adds up to $204,120; the lender makes $104,120 off of you. Yes, the monthly payments are lower with a 30-year loan, but over the long haul you've paid more than twice as much interest.

Another point to consider with loan terms is the amount that goes to principal and interest each month. With fixed-rate mortgages, most of the initial payments go to interest, with very little going to principal. But when the loan term is shortened, say from 30 years to 15, you also pay down your principal more quickly.

Using the same information as in the previous example, after 5 years the loan balance on the 30-year loan is $92,316. You've paid down your original mortgage only $7,684. With the 15-year loan, your balance is $74,076, a difference of $18,240 after just 5 years.

There's a trade-off with amortization. Lower payments also mean slower loan paydown. Fixed-rate loans can also have another feature called a *balloon*. With a balloon, the loan comes due in full after a predetermined period has elapsed. Many conventional loans with balloons come due after five years and are called "thirty-due-in-five," written as "30/5." Again using the previous example, after five years your loan balance of $92,316 becomes due, all of it, to the lender. The loan has to be refinanced or paid off in some other way to avoid the balloon payment. Who would want a balloon payment?

Lenders offer balloons because they can offer a reduced interest rate. And these loans are particularly attractive if borrowers don't think they'll have the mortgage that long anyway. The interest rate on a 30/5 might be 5.25 percent instead of 5.55 percent.

There's another version of a fixed-rate loan, sometimes called a "two-step" or a 5/25. This loan offers a reduced initial rate for 5 years, then makes a one-time adjustment to another rate for the remaining 25 years. There are also two-step loans called 7/23s that work similarly.

Adjustable Rates

Adjustable-rate mortgages, or ARMs, adjust. The rate changes. Fortunately for you, there's a rhyme and a reason to both when and how much it changes. There are ARMs where the rate changes twice per year, once per year, once per month, and so on. The ARM you choose will have preset change options built into the note, and those change options are called the index, margin, and cap.

The *index* is the benchmark your adjustable-rate mortgage is associated with or tied to. The one-year Treasury note and a six-month CD are common indexes, but the index can be just about anything the lender wants it to be. Other common indexes are the prime rate, the six-month Treasury bill rate, and the London Interbank Offered Rate, or LIBOR.

The second component of an ARM is the *margin*. Think "profit margin" and you'll get the idea. The margin is the amount that is added to the previously agreed-upon index to arrive at your interest rate.

For example, suppose your ARM is based on the six-month Treasury bill rate. On the date your note is set, that index, which can fluctuate with the economy, might be 3.61 percent. Next add your margin (a common one is 2.75 percent) to the index of 3.61 percent, and the interest rate that will be used in calculating your monthly payments is 2.75 + 3.61 or 6.36 percent. When does your rate adjust next?

The *adjustment period* is another feature of an ARM. This is the exact date on which your loan is adjusted. The lender will take the index at the time of the adjustment and add the margin. Often the adjustment time coincides with the index used in the ARM. If your index is a one-year

Treasury note, then your loan might adjust once per year, every year. If the index is a six-month CD, your rate might adjust every six months. But this isn't necessarily true for all ARMs; it's just how most operate.

But what happens, you may ask, if your index goes from 2.50 percent in Year 1 to 10.00 percent in Year 2? That means a big change in payments, right? Wrong. Built into your ARM are neat consumer things called *adjustment caps* or just *caps*. A cap protects you from index mood swings. Most caps are 1 percent every six months or 2 percent per year. But not all are that way. Government ARMs, for example, have a 1 percent cap every 12 months.

Okay, back to our example. Your index started at 2.00 percent, and when your 2.50 percent margin was added, your mortgage rate was a whopping 4.50 percent. For a $200,000 30-year loan, that works out to a monthly payment of $1,013. But weird things happened over the next year, and your index rose significantly, to 10.00 percent. Now when you add your 2.50 percent margin, your new rate is 12.50 percent, resulting in a new monthly payment of $2,134 per month—more than twice what you were paying.

But because you had an adjustment cap of 2 percent, your interest rate can never be more than 2 percentage points higher or lower than the previous year's rate. So even though your ARM wanted to go to 12.50 percent, it couldn't do so because of the cap. It could go up only 2 percentage points, to 6.50 percent. Now your payment adjusts to $1,264. This is higher than before, but nothing like what you would have had without an adjustment cap.

Another type of cap is the *lifetime cap*, or the highest rate your loan can ever get to. Most caps are 6.00 percent over the rate you started at, so in this example your rate would never be higher than 4.50 + 6.00, or 10.50 percent. Yeah, that's high, but it took three years to get there.

Why do some people take ARMs, and why do other people take fixed-rate loans? Generally speaking, a borrower will select an ARM if fixed rates are much higher and interest rates are at historical or cyclical highs. This means that based on recent history and economic trends, the odds of rates in general going lower are greater than the odds of their going higher.

People who don't plan to own a home for very long might also choose an ARM. People who choose a fixed rate do so when rates are at historical lows or when they plan on owning the home for a very long time.

Hybrids

There's also an "in-between" choice. It's called a hybrid. A *hybrid* is a cross between a fixed-rate loan and an ARM in that the rate is fixed for a preset period, but then the loan turns into an annual or semiannual ARM. Common hybrid forms are fixed for five years, then turning into a one-year annual ARM (called a 5/1) or fixed for seven years, then again turning into a one-year annual ARM (called a 7/1).

Hybrids can also morph into six-month ARMS or have different initial rates. If you can figure out what a 5/6 ARM or a 3/1 ARM is, then you get the picture. Why choose a hybrid?

Hybrids are more popular among people who are fairly certain that they're not going to have the mortgage for very long. If a home buyer is certain that she is going to be transferred at her job within five years, she might choose a 5/1 or 5/6 ARM. The rates are lower than on a standard 30-year fixed-rate loan, and she avoids the annual adjustments that can occur with ARMs. In fact, hybrids have become the loan program du jour for short-termers.

Another type of ARM that has gained fame is called an interest-only loan. With this type of program, the monthly payment is established using simple interest only. Simple interest is interest accrued daily, with no preset amortization period. The interest rate is applied to the loan balance to get the dollar amount owed. To calculate an interest-only loan for a mortgage, multiply the rate and the loan amount. The result is the annual amount of interest due on the loan. Now divide that amount by 12 (months in a year) to arrive at your payment for an interest-only loan.

When you compare a fully amortized loan to an interest-only loan, the difference is noticeable. Again using the 30-year fixed-rate example given earlier, a 5.5 percent interest-only payment on $100,000 is 5.5% × $100,000 = $5,500. Divide that amount by 12 and the monthly payment is $458. Compare that with the fully amortized payment of $567 at 5.50 percent and you can really see the difference. When you hear or read mortgage advertisements declaring how much some loan company can reduce your monthly payment, it's usually the interest-only program that you're hearing about.

Remember how we compared the difference in loan balance between a 30-year and a 15-year loan? Now let's compare the difference in loan balance for an interest-only loan. After five years of paying $458 per month, you've paid absolutely nothing toward the original loan balance. It's the same. It has to be—you've paid "interest only."

Take an interest-only loan only after careful consideration. These loans may have their place, but if you're using an interest-only loan for the sole purpose of getting your payment down so that you can qualify, you may be setting yourself up for a disaster.

During the early 2000s, it seemed that almost every real estate transaction turned to gold. With record low interest rates combined with a recovering economy, people were lining up to buy houses. With such demand, naturally home values increased. When home values increase, homeowners accrue equity not by paying down the loan and regaining their principal, but by the appreciation in home prices resulting from market demand.

But what if homes don't appreciate? Home prices can sometimes go down, just as they can go up. Just as one can gain equity solely as a result of market conditions, one can also lose equity as a result of market conditions. If you choose an interest-only loan and don't pay anything toward the principal, and simultaneously real estate prices are falling, you're hit with a double-whammy. You could soon be "upside down" with the property—owing much more than the home is worth.

Interest-only loans have a positive side for those who both gain from appreciation and are financially capable of paying down the principal on a regular basis. They are also popular among real estate investors who buy property to rent and are looking for a positive cash flow. Interest-only loans can also be used by those who get seasonal or irregular income, where bulk payments can be made toward the loan as money is earned throughout the year.

Option ARMS and Negative Amortization

A new twist, or, rather, a renamed twist, on ARMs is sometimes called the *option ARM*. An option ARM is a loan program where the borrower has an option, in fact several options, about how much to pay on the loan each month.

Sounds neat, doesn't it, to have an option as to how much to pay your mortgage company? Option ARMs do in fact give you a choice of payment terms each month. The choices usually are:

- The minimum monthly payment as required by your note
- An interest-only payment based upon the index plus margin
- A fully amortized payment

The potential trap with these loans is that while it's nice to make only a 1 percent payment each month (if that's what's on the original contract), if you don't make at least the fully indexed payment, then the difference gets added onto the original loan amount. Let's take an example.

The loan amount is $400,000, the minimum payment each month is 1 percent, and the fully indexed payment is 5.00 percent. A simple interest 1 percent on $400,000 is $333, while the fully indexed rate at 5.00 percent is $1,667. If the borrower has the option of paying either amount but chooses the 1 percent, the remaining amount, $1,667 − $333, or $1,334, gets added to the original loan amount.

In the olden days, before electricity or running water, this aspect of an option loan was called "negative amortization." The borrower could elect to pay a lower amount than the fully indexed rate or the fully amortized rate, but the difference would get added back to the loan, amortizing negatively. Amortizing negatively is a nice way of saying that the loan actually gets bigger as one pays it, not smaller.

Apparently the term *negative amortization* had too much negative connotation, so lenders changed it to an "option." Well, this option can get scary. Here's another part of the option ARM that many people don't know about: If the loan balance grows to 25 percent above the original loan, all bets are off and the loan turns into a fully amortized fixed-rate loan. Ouch. If someone gets comfortable with either the minimum monthly payment or the interest-only payment, then suddenly gets hit with a fully indexed one, that can mean foreclosure. There are simply too many financing options for someone to choose instead of one of these loans.

However, if you completely understand interest-only loans or option ARMs and know how they work, you should consider them. Real estate investors like them because they can keep their monthly payments low while using the difference in payment to invest in other things, such as more real estate, stocks, or other investment vehicles.

There are places for option ARMs, and those places might again be for those who get paid infrequently or who plan on keeping a property only for a very short period, but using an option ARM in order to qualify for the mortgage in the first place is irresponsible behavior on the part of the loan officer and a very bad mistake for the consumer. There are simply too many choices in the mortgage market without having to resort to a loan program that inherently has potential foreclosure built right into it. Especially when the borrower has done nothing wrong, and has paid the amount required by the note.

CHAPTER 4

The Mortgage Application Process

Now that you know the major play-
ers and have a general overview of the process, you are ready to take the
first step: filling out an application. Ideally, you are filling out the application before you go shopping for a home. This way, you know how much
you can afford, and you are armed with a prequalification letter. A prequalification letter strengthens an offer when you make one. It shows
that you can actually come through with the financing if the seller accepts
your offer. Prequalification and preapproval are also stages of loan accep-
tance. A *prequalification* for a mortgage loan means that, based on what
the mortgage applicant said or put on his loan application, he would
qualify for a mortgage. It's far from being a loan approval, and you need
to take prequalifications with a grain of salt. Or two. Prequalifications
really don't mean all that much, except as a verification that yes, you
spoke to a loan officer, but no, the loan officer didn't verify anything on
your application, much less review a credit report. In fact, very few Realtors even accept a prequalification letter.

The next stage of approval is one step past prequalification, or verification of the information on the application and reviewing a credit report. The credit report will tell the loan officer whether the person does
or doesn't have good credit. Along with the officer's having reviewed the
credit report, a *preapproval* should also mean that the application has
been reviewed and might even have been input into an AUS. But addi-

tional levels of verification still haven't been performed; specifically, the lender hasn't received income tax returns, paycheck stubs, or rental verification. However, preapprovals are close. Many Realtors accept a preapproval letter.

The final stage would be a pure approval. A loan approval, sometimes called a *commitment*, means that everything pertinent to the borrower's ability to repay a mortgage and be approved for a loan has been reviewed. The credit report is satisfactory; the loan has been submitted to an AUS; and employment, asset, and credit history have been verified.

This is the approval letter that Realtors want to see.

If you've already found a property, that's OK, too. A mortgage application is still the first step, and it will help you figure out which type of loan you qualify for.

The mortgage application, sometimes called the 1003 (ten-oh-three) because that's the Fannie Mae form number, is your first step in getting approved. Before you go shopping for a home, you will have applied for a home loan by completing this form. Unless you already have a property picked out, you won't know certain key elements, such as the sales price, loan type, or property address, but you'll still need to complete this form first. It's your road map. If you have credit or income issues, your loan officer will need to know about any problems at the outset and guide you in the proper direction. Filling out a loan application is the only way to really know where you are and how lenders will look at your loan.

The loan application is about five pages long using legal-sized paper, and there are about 1,000 boxes to fill in. Okay, that's an exaggeration; there are closer to 250 boxes to fill in. However, it's not as intimidating as one would think at first glance. It's divided into 10 sections, but they all revolve around two things: you and the property.

The 10 sections are:

1. Type of mortgage and loan terms
2. Property information and purpose of loan
3. Borrower information
4. Employment information

5. Monthly income and housing expense information
6. Assets and liabilities
7. Details of transaction
8. Declarations
9. Acknowledgment and agreement
10. Information for government monitoring purposes

Type of Mortgage and Loan Terms

At the very top of your application, this section asks you what type of mortgage loan you're looking for: a conventional loan, an FHA or VA loan, a USDA loan, or some other type. Most of the time, the borrower hasn't decided on which type of loan is best. For preapproval purposes, you don't need to know right now which loan type you'll end up with. You should make an educated guess, however, and you can modify it later if necessary. Loan officers can help you decide which program is ideal, but here are some general guidelines:

- If you have the money for a down payment and closing costs, a conventional loan is usually the most competitive.
- If you are a veteran, there are loans open to you that waive the down payment and closing cost requirements. If you don't have the money for these, this is likely to be your best bet. If, on the other hand, you do have the money, you should probably start with a conventional loan because those rates tend to be more competitive.

Keep in mind that whatever you decide now, you can change your mind later. Heck, you could change your mind several times and it wouldn't be that big a deal. But unless your loan application is the "bread and butter" variety with 20 percent down, it's likely that you won't know which type of loan you'll ultimately be applying for. If you're not sure, leave it blank and let your loan officer decide. For example, if you're a qualifying veteran, your loan officer will probably first explore VA loans.

If you're living in a rural area and qualify for a USDA loan, the loan officer will also research the USDA option along with FHA loans. Other times, none of these choices will apply; then your loan officer will simply select "Other" and move on.

This section probably helps the lender more than the borrower. When FHA or VA is checked, other documents specific to a government loan will be generated.

You'll also be asked to check either "fixed" or "adjustable" mortgage. As discussed in Chapter 3, a fixed rate is just that—the interest rate is fixed for the term of the loan. Adjustable-rate loans tend to start with lower interest rates than fixed-rate loans and increase or decrease at regular intervals as time goes on. If you think interest rates will go down, or that your income will increase enough to cover the increased interest rates, an adjustable-rate mortgage might be the best option for you. Some people also choose adjustable because they think they will move before the rate goes up. These are some of the issues you will need to consider when comparing loans.

Remember that if you're not sure right now which type of mortgage you're likely to want, you can change your mind or skip a section if you want.

Property Information and Purpose of Loan

This section asks for vital information such as the address of the property and its legal description. Odds are that you won't know the legal description, which is typically something like "Block 2, Lot 4, Sunshine Subdivision Phase IV." Your attorney or title report will typically provide these data. You'll complete this section only if you've already found a home to buy. If you haven't, then the lender will fill this part out for you.

Is the loan for a purchase, are you refinancing, or are you building a brand new home? This area also asks whether you're buying the property to live in or are going to rent it out. Is it a vacation home? A second home? You'll check that in Section 2.

Another important feature of Section 2 is who will legally be owning the property in terms of holding title to the real estate. Husband and wife as joint tenants? A single woman as sole owner? There are various legal ways in which people can own property, and these can also vary under state law. If you're in doubt or concerned about the differences, ask for some quick legal advice. If you're married, you'll most likely take title as joint tenants, meaning that should one spouse die, the other spouse automatically gets the house without going through probate. If you're a single man, then that's an easy one: unmarried man, sole owner, for example.

And a final piece of Section 2 asks, "Okay, where are you getting the money for this deal, anyway?" Okay, not in such plain language as that; it's a tad more formal, but that's the essence of it.

Borrower Information

Here's the good stuff. Here is where you put your name, your social security number, your telephone number, where you live, your date of birth, and even how many years of school you've had. That last one sounds a little goofy. I've never seen a loan turned down because some-one didn't go to enough classes, but it's been around for years. Probably one of these years that question about whether or not you went to college or finished high school will be removed. Personally, I think it has little, if any, bearing.

This area also asks where you've lived for the past two years, and whether you've owned or rented. If you've owned before, the dates you put down on the application should match the dates that appear on your credit report if you got a mortgage. If you've rented, the application will ask for the name and phone number of whomever you sent your rental payments to. Your lender will want to verify a payment history.

If you're borrowing with someone else, married or not, the co-borrower will put his or her information alongside yours. If there's some-thing that you're not sure about, come back to it later or talk to your loan officer about it. But really, this section is fairly straightforward.

Employment Information

This section asks for information about your job: where you work, the name of the company, and whether or not you own your own business. In this section, how you're paid is established, and this tells the lender how to document your loan file. Self-employed people will typically provide tax returns, while those who are on someone else's payroll will provide only W2 stubs from the previous couple of years.

This section also asks not only where you work but also what you do there. If you work for a manufacturer, are you a chemical engineer or a maintenance engineer? Do you work in the accounting department? In sales? You'll also be asked not only how long you've worked for your current employer, but also how long you've worked in that type of job.

Have you been at your current employer for less than two years? Are you newly self-employed? Then the lender will also want some information about your previous job, so be prepared to provide information on your previous employer, such as name, address, and phone number for verification purposes and how much money you made there.

Monthly Income and Housing Expense Information

Okay, friend. Here's the money part. There are separate areas for different types of income: one for standard wages, another for overtime, one for bonuses and commissions, another for dividends and interest income, and still others for rental income and the now-famous "other" category.

Don't let this section intimidate you. I've had borrowers turn glum when they see how many different types of income are being asked for, mistakenly thinking that lenders expect a borrower to have more than one source of income. Some certainly do, but by a wide margin most people get income from one single source: their employer. Maybe there will be some overtime wages, or maybe someone in sales gets commissions or a bonus check, but most people have just one paycheck.

Right next door to this section is a place for present housing expense and proposed housing expense. In this area, you put your monthly rental payment if you rent or your payment for principal and interest, taxes, and insurance if you currently own a house and have a mortgage on it. Note that the "proposed" section is based upon your new purchase and will include everything in your payment, along with mortgage insurance, homeowner's insurance, property taxes, and any homeowner's association dues.

The figures in Section 5 are what your "debt ratios" are based on. We'll discuss how debt ratios are calculated in Chapter 5.

Assets and Liabilities

This is the lengthiest part of the application, but again, don't worry if you don't fill in every blank. This area lists all your liquid and nonliquid assets, such as checking and savings accounts, money market funds, mutual funds or stock, and retirement accounts such as 401(k)s and IRAs.

The trick here is to be accurate, but if you're not sure about an account number or an exact balance, then certainly don't worry about it. Your loan officer will document those sources later on anyway. But for purposes of the application, this gives your lender an idea of which loan options will be available to you.

Here too there are some old questions that still linger on the 1003, asking about furniture and jewelry. Several years ago, lenders would add up your assets and compare them to your liabilities to arrive at a "net worth" number. Now, however, net worth is rarely addressed, so don't worry too much about these questions.

On the right-hand side of this section is where you list your liabilities: your car payment, your credit card debt, your student loans, child support. If you're not sure about a particular balance or an account number, either just estimate it or wait until your credit report is pulled. At that point, all account numbers will appear alongside the associated balances and monthly payments.

The end of Section 6 lets you list rental properties or other real estate that you own. Again, don't be intimidated by this. It's nothing more than gathering data about you so that the lender can determine which type of loans would work best for you.

Details of Transaction

The sales price, your down payment, your closing costs, and any money you've given as a down payment will be shown here. Almost every time I've seen Section 7 of the loan application completed by the borrower, it's always been just a little bit wrong because this section is so confusing. It's so confusing that even your loan officer will have trouble explaining it. And it's also fluid. Each time you change something, such as a closing cost, an interest rate, or the down payment amount, this section will change. The only time it will be completely correct just might be at your closing. If it's off, though, it'll usually be off by only a few dollars.

Declarations

Here's the section where you cross your heart that you didn't lie about anything on your application. It asks things such as, "Have you been bankrupt?" and "Have you been foreclosed upon?" and "Do you intend to occupy the property as your primary residence?" Just answer the questions honestly.

We'll discuss loan fraud and what happens when people don't tell the truth on the loan application in Chapter 7. Trust me, it's not pretty.

Acknowledgment and Agreement

Here you're asked yet again, in essence, "Have you told the truth?" You're also acknowledging things such as understanding that the lender will contact other people to verify parts of your application, understanding that if your loan goes bad, the lender can foreclose, and so on. This section is in very, very small type. Maybe that's why all of these questions are asked yet again, more than twice, on other loan papers and disclosure forms. There are no less than 11 different declarations that you agree to in this section. That's a lot. You ought to read it.

Information for Government Monitoring Purposes

In this final section, you check different boxes stating whether you are male or female and also list your nationality, such as Hispanic or Latino, black, Asian, and so on. It also gives you a little box that says, "I don't wish to tell you my race or sex."

Some people see this area and get suspicious. They think, "I'm not going to put down that I'm this or that so they won't discriminate against me. I want the lender to make a lending decision that has nothing to do with my race or whether I'm a guy or a girl." Actually, this information doesn't go to lenders. With the advent of automated underwriting systems, lenders have no clue as to race or sex when loans are submitted through an AUS. You're being approved by a computer program. The program doesn't take race or sex into account.

The reason this box is here is so that the government can monitor lending patterns. If you don't answer these questions, the government can't track whether one group of people gets more loans than another.

There. Your loan application is complete.

CHAPTER 5

Debt Ratios and
How They're Calculated

A debt ratio is like any other ratio. It's one number as a percentage of another. Debt ratios for purposes of buying a home typically include two numbers, sometimes called your *front*, or *housing*, ratio and your *back*, or *total debt*, ratio

Your front ratio takes into account your principal and interest payment plus your monthly property tax bill and monthly insurance payment. It also includes any monthly mortgage insurance premium you're paying and any homeowner's association dues if the property is a condominium or part of some other type of planned development.

For instance, suppose you borrow $200,000 at a 30-year fixed rate of 7.00 percent. The principal and interest payment is $1,330. Now take your annual property tax bill and divide it by 12. If your annual taxes are $2,000 per year, then your monthly tax payment would be $2,000 divided by 12, or $167. Take your annual homeowner's insurance premium and divide it, too, by 12. In this example, your premium might be $1,000, so your monthly insurance premium would be $83.

Your housing payment adds up to $1,580. Note that many people do not make monthly tax and insurance payments, sometimes called *escrow* or *impound* account payments. Regardless of whether you pay taxes and insurance monthly or annually, for the purposes of calculating debt ratios, the lender will add principal and interest, taxes, and insurance plus any mortgage insurance or homeowner's dues.

To arrive at the front ratio, divide your total house payment by your gross monthly income. This is gross income, mind you—the income number used before any taxes or withholdings are removed. If your gross monthly income is $5,000, then your front ratio would be $1,580 divided by $5,000, or 0.316. Your front ratio is 31.6 percent.

For the back ratio or total ratio, add up all revolving and installment consumer debt. Also don't forget to include other monthly obligations, such as child support or student loans.

Let's take an automobile payment of $450, two credit card payments totaling $200 per month, and some student loan payments adding up to $150 per month. That's a total of $800. There are some particulars that you need to consider when calculating your debt ratios. First, use only the minimum required monthly payment on your credit card or installment loans when figuring ratios. You may pay $500 per month on a credit card, but the minimum amount required as per the card statement is $50.

Lenders also dismiss any installment loan that has less than 10 months remaining. If your car loan has eight months left before it is paid off in full, then you don't have to count that additional $450 in your debt ratio calculation.

When you add the $800 number to your housing payment of $1,580, you get $2,380. Again divide that number by your gross monthly income of $5,000 and you get 0.476, or 47.6 percent. Your debt ratios are 31.6/47.6. If a loan requires ratios of 40/50, then your ratios are below the allowable limits, and you will qualify.

If a loan requires 28/38, then you may not qualify. Or if the allowable ratios are 38/44, then you would qualify on the front but not on the back. Some loans have very strict ratio requirements, while most others are simply "guidelines." In this instance, you should certainly pay attention to the debt ratios, but by all means don't fail to apply for the loan just because a number is 43 when it should be 42.

Calculating debt ratios is important, but whatever you do, don't "decline" yourself by not applying for a mortgage just because you think your ratios are too high. I've seen too many people sit on the sidelines because they've gone to a web site somewhere, read about debt ratios and what they need to be or not be, and then never applied. Ratios are typically a rule of thumb, not a hard-and-fast rule. Don't get me wrong, debt ratios are important; they give the underwriter a fair idea of whether or not you can afford the monthly payments. But let the lender decide whether your ratio fits into its program.

Typical housing ratios are somewhere between 28 and 33. Typical total debt ratios are between 38 and 45. But that's only for standard debt ratios. Several years ago, an underwriter might have declined a loan because a housing ratio was above 45, for example. Now, with advanced underwriting software, ratios are no longer so strictly enforced.

Calculating Income

When determining debt ratios, it's important to know how your lender will calculate your income. That can depend on whether you're paid by the hour, the day, the week, or for some other period.

Some people don't get paid that way, and they have special income issues. For example, some people get paid once a month and some every other week, and that's not even counting the self-employed borrower who gets paid whenever the business happens to make some money. Knowing how your income will be calculated will help you determine how much money you can borrow.

For those who are paid by the hour, lenders want to see that hourly income be full-time. A 40-hour workweek is considered full-time, but most guidelines will ask for only a minimum of 36 hours to consider your work full-time. Anything less is considered part-time and has special rules of its own.

If you work 40 hours per week and get paid $20 per hour, then you make $800 per week. But lenders don't use weekly income, they use monthly income, so don't be tricked by multiplying that $800 times four weeks. There are actually 4.33 weeks per month if you average it out over the entire year—and your lender will do just that.

Instead of taking your weekly income and multiplying it by 4.33, your lender will take your weekly income of $800, multiply it by all 52 weeks in the year, then divide by 12. That number is your gross income for purposes of calculating ratios.

$$\$800 \times 52 \text{ weeks} = \$41{,}600 \div 12 \text{ months} = \$3{,}467 \text{ per month}$$

Do you get overtime? There are special rules for overtime, but those rules are consistent with the rules for other types of income. You must have a consistent history of overtime work, meaning that you can prove that you had overtime income during the previous two years and that the overtime income is likely to continue.

It's easy to prove overtime income over the past two years; your lender will calculate your regular earnings, then subtract them from your total income. If you made $61,600 in each of the previous two years, the lender will subtract your regular income of $41,600, leaving $20,000. The lender will divide that again by 12, giving you another $1,667 per month, and add that to your gross income of $3,467. Your total income is then $5,134.

So how does an underwriter determine that overtime is likely to continue? First, the lender will try to get your employer to say so; in fact, the lender can send a form asking just that. If the employer is unwilling to do that, and many are, the lender will simply make a judgment call. If it gets to this point and you have a track record, your overtime earnings will most likely be used.

Part-time income can also be used, but only under certain conditions. As with overtime, you must show a track record of part-time earnings over a two-year period, and you must show that you currently are earning income from that same part-time source. If you've worked part-time at the same job for a couple of years and are still working there, your part-time income will be counted. If you no longer work there, then it won't be counted.

If you work part-time at different jobs, your lender might consider that only if you can prove you've been doing both jobs over two years and are still doing so.

Commission income also requires a two-year history and average. If you're new to commissions and you made $5,000 two years ago and $50,000 last year, the lender won't use the $50,000, but instead will average the two years. In this case, the $55,000 would be divided by 24 months to arrive at $2,291 per month.

Your year-to-date commission earnings are also added to this average. If qualifying on $2,291 doesn't seem too appetizing, then hopefully your year-to-date income will help. If it's June 30 and you've made $60,000 so far this year, the lender will add the $55,000 to the $60,000, then divide by the 30 months used to earn that income. Now your income used to qualify is nearly doubled, to $3,833.

If you're self-employed, your lender will use the income from your tax returns. Specifically, it will take your previous two years' tax returns and average them. If you're a sole proprietor, your lender will take your business income and subtract your business expenses, and presto, the result is your qualifying income.

Here's where it gets a little dicey for some businesses. Many business owners can run everyday, legitimate expenses through their business and deduct them from their business income. Less income means less income tax, right? But if too many expenses are written off to avoid taxes, then the business owner is hit with a lower income for purposes of calculating ratios.

Let's say you run a restaurant and gross $200,000 per year. Not bad. But by the time you deduct rent, salaries, food, utilities, insurance, and company vehicles, your income is reduced by $180,000, giving you a gross annual income of $20,000. Your lender will use $1,667 per month to underwrite you regardless of how much money your business took in.

Loan Documentation: Proving Your Income

So, with all these choices of documentation levels, why not just choose the easiest method and get on with one's life without all the hassle of loan paperwork? There are a couple of reasons: rate and term.

Lenders don't like surprises. They want everything laid out in front of them so that they can make an informed lending decision. Debt ratios, down payment requirements, employment history—all of these are part of a track record that can steer a lender toward making the correct decision.

When a borrower protects something about his application or otherwise doesn't fully disclose, the lender is now faced with an added element of risk. If a lender encounters greater risk, then guess what? The lender must offset that risk by either increasing the interest rate on a particular transaction, lowering the allowable debt ratios, or requiring more money down from the borrower.

Many AUS applications automatically apply such risk adjustments when making a loan decision by asking for less documentation for loans that apparently have lower risk. But when loans get past the conventional stage and enter the world of stated or no documentation (discussed later in this chapter), then risk balance is introduced.

Documentation levels should be considered on a case-by-case basis.

If you'd rather not produce the mounds of data the lender wants to see and you are willing to take the additional hit in interest rate, then by all means do it. That's why lenders issue such loans. But if you're providing less or no documentation simply because the documentation doesn't exist or because you're faking some income—don't do it. Your new home could be an 8 × 8 cell in a prison.

Why do people need different amounts of documentation? The reasons vary. It can be simply "I don't feel like supplying all of that documentation," or borrower's convenience. Or it can be that the borrower's income or assets don't meet the lender's guidelines.

For example, a common requirement for a fully documented loan for someone who is self-employed is verification that the borrower has been in business for more than two years. If the borrower hasn't been in business for that long, he needs to find a loan type that his employment situation allows him to qualify for. In this case, the answer may be a "no doc" loan.

Some loan programs require certain assets to have been in an account for a particular period of time, called "seasoning." If a borrower's assets don't meet a particular seasoning requirement but are still available to buy the home, then the borrower would apply for a "stated asset" loan.

When it comes to income, lenders also have guidelines that they must use when underwriting a fully documented file. They must verify that income not only has a two-year history but also has a "likelihood of continuance." It's this likelihood that borrowers sometimes can't provide. A common example might be disability income. Sometimes a lender will ask the borrower's doctor to provide an opinion regarding the disability and whether it will continue for two years or more. The doctor may not know or may not care to answer. In a fully documented file, that income couldn't be used to qualify the borrower. In this situation, a "stated income" or "no income" file could be approved.

If you have any difficulty in qualifying because of your assets, income, or employment history, then perhaps you just haven't found the right type of loan.

I've heard on more than one occasion that lenders expect you to lie when you apply for a "stated" loan. That's a crock. Lenders do no such thing. That's also a word of caution. If your loan officer tells you what you need to put on your application, and it's not true, then you both have committed loan fraud. If you get a loan officer who tells you to leave much of your application blank so that she can fill it in later, be very careful. If the loan officer fills out the application with information that isn't true, you could be liable. If you don't trust your loan officer, get a new one.

Loan Documentation

Loan documentation is a form of verification. And verification comes in all shapes and sizes. Some lenders have their own names for documentation verification status, but most in the industry have accepted a few standard names for documentation that mean the same thing to everyone else. Loan documentation comes in the following formats:

Full documentation

Alternate documentation

Stated documentation

Stated income documentation

Stated asset documentation

No income documentation

No asset documentation

No income, no asset documentation

No employment documentation

No documentation

Why would lenders offer so many variations on documenting a loan? Lenders are like any other business; they can market mortgage loans the way any other company might market any other product. Lenders can differentiate themselves by doing things differently, or at least appearing to do so. Have you seen television commercials where lenders brag about how little documentation they need? That's a marketing tool. Sometimes less documentation is for borrower convenience, and sometimes it's a borrower necessity.

Full Documentation

With full documentation, or "full doc," everything about the borrower is verified. This verification comes in written, third-party form. If the borrower states on the application that he makes $5,000 per month, the lender won't simply take his word for it. Instead, it sends his employer a Verification of Employment letter, or VOE, which asks the employer to fill out a questionnaire asking, first, does this person work there, and if so, how long has he worked there and how much does he make?

A full documentation loan is typically verified through the mail. Some underwriters (those who have been around for a few years and still have some old habits to break) will actually run their fingers over the VOE to see if it has any creases. If it did, the VOE was, in fact, folded, then mailed in an envelope.

Full documentation for employment also means providing paycheck stubs covering the most recent 30-day period and maybe even the previous two years' W2 forms.

Full documentation for assets means that a Verification of Deposit form, or VOD, was mailed to and completed by a financial institution. Or the most recent three months' worth of statements are provided. Borrowers can even provide a printout of an online bank or investment statement as long as the statement has not just the borrower's name but also part of his social security number and account number, with the accompanying URL address shown at the top or bottom of the printout.

Full documentation for rental or mortgage history can come from a credit report or through 12 months' cancelled checks showing timely payment. In full documentation, nothing gets accepted without being verified by someone who is not the borrower or related to the borrower.

Alternate Documentation

Alternate documentation, or "alt doc," has changed its meaning over the years, with the massive spread of stated and low documentation loans. Alt doc primarily means any type of documentation other than full doc, but typically it means a verbal verification instead of a written one. In the case of a verbal verification, most often the loan processor makes a phone call to the employer and goes over a questionnaire, asking questions such as, "Does he work there?" and "How much money does he make?" Alt doc can also mean bank statements instead of a VOD.

Stated Documentation

Stated doc means that the lender will use what the borrower puts on the application without any verification whatsoever. If a borrower says that she makes $10,000 per month, then that's what the underwriter will use when determining debt ratios. If she says that she makes $100,000 per month, that's the number the underwriter will work with.

A bit of common sense is needed with stated doc loans. If someone puts down that she makes $100,000 per year but lists her occupation as a store clerk, then the underwriter might ask for some additional documentation or require her to make sense of the income in some other way.

One way in which lenders "verify" a stated doc loan is by asking for verification of other assets or for a particular credit score. Some stated doc loans require a larger down payment or charge a higher rate.

A real-world example of a stated doc loan is a loan that requires three months' worth of stated income in a liquid account. If the borrower puts down $100,000 per month as his income, the lender would ask to see $300,000 in cash or liquid accounts. Does this make sense? It should. Someone who makes a particular level of income should have a reasonable amount of assets relative to that income. If someone makes $3,000 per month, then it would be likely that this person also has $9,000 in checking, savings, or 401(k) accounts. Verifying assets is a "back door" way of verifying income.

Stated doc loans can also be used by those who don't wish to verify their assets, for whatever reason. I recall a client who made a whole lot of money. I mean, a *whole* lot. He owned two construction companies and had invested in more general partnerships than you could count. His tax returns were at least six inches thick. If he had applied on a full doc basis, then the underwriter would have no choice but to verify each and every item submitted. Since he owned so many different companies, he would have had to provide a set of tax returns on each to verify business income. There was no need to "beat him up" with paperwork on all his various businesses, so instead he applied for a stated doc loan.

Still another client liked to diversify her assets. Many people have more than one investment or retirement account, but this lady had 28. For a full doc loan, she would have had to provide three months' most recent investment statements for all 28 accounts. Think for a moment about one of your 401(k) statements, or maybe a statement from a mutual fund. How many pages are there? Several, right? This client would have had to produce over 100 pages of asset documentation simply because that's what she put on her application.

Stated Income Documentation

Stated income loans use the income put on the loan application for purposes of determining debt ratios but verify everything else on the application, including assets, employment, and anything else that the lender wants to verify.

Stated Asset Documentation

Stated asset loans use the assets as stated in the loan application but verify everything else on the application. Assets are used for the down payment and closing costs, and lenders need to see if a borrower has enough money to close a transaction. Stated assets don't go through the "provide three months' most recent statements" drill.

No Income Documentation

Here's a twist on the stated income loan. For this loan type, no income information whatsoever is put on the application. Hence no ratios are calculated, but everything else is verified. Most no income loans have fairly steep asset, credit, or down payment requirements.

No Asset Documentation

This type of loan is the same as no income doc, but with no assets listed on the application. The lender assumes that the borrower has enough money to close the transaction without verifying it. Income is verified along with other verifiable facets of the loan.

No Income, No Asset Documentation

This type of loan is also called a "nina," for no income no asset. No income information is put on the application, and no tax returns or pay stubs are provided. From an asset standpoint, absolutely no bank or investment statements are provided. Everything else is verified, including employment and credit history.

No Employment Documentation

Nothing with regard to employment is listed on the application, but everything else is verified.

No Documentation

This term is used too often in the lending industry. As a matter of fact, a true no doc loan is rare. No employment, no income, and no assets are used to approve the loan. The only requirements are a credit history and showing up at the closing table with enough money to close.

Hard-to-Prove Income

Okay, so you have "hard-to-prove" income. How do you qualify for that home loan? This usually means that your income doesn't quite fit lenders' guidelines. That can mean:

The income doesn't have a two-year history.

The income isn't likely to continue for two to three years.

The income can't be documented by third-party sources.

Note that none of these three requirements mean that you're trying to fool the underwriter. They don't mean that the income doesn't exist. Why would anyone go through all the hassle of buying a home without any means of paying the note? However, an underwriter is required to document a loan so that it fits the lender's requirements. Lenders look for a history of income, and if you can't prove a source of income, it most likely won't be counted. But that's why there are stated loans. Here are a few examples of real income that lenders may or may not accept on a full doc basis:

An artist selling her first paintings

A ballplayer getting his first paycheck playing baseball

A businessperson opening up a successful new car-wash business

A single parent working two or even three jobs to try to pay for college

A chef opening a new restaurant

A person whose income is from a pension

An author whose new book is selling like crazy

A general contractor who gets income on a job-to-job basis

A "handyman" who roves about getting odd jobs

All of these endeavors are worthy, but sometimes in the eyes of lenders, the income just can't be counted. It's not that the income isn't there;

it's just that the loans are reserved for those whose paychecks come twice per month or who are paid by the hour. Hourly or monthly wages reported on a W2 are easy to verify. Other income sources may not be.

So what do you do if your income falls outside of the standard guidelines? Most stated loans have a guideline that's nearly impossible to get around: the two-year history of employment. Almost any type of loan can be approved under various credit standards, but the need to have a most-recent-two-year history of employment or self-employment is usually rock-solid. So how do you verify two years of employment if you're going stated?

If you're self-employed or get income from different sources, a lender will ask for a letter from your CPA stating how long you've been doing what you've been doing. If you don't have an accountant or some other third party who can verify your most recent two years, then a copy of your business license with a date on it will work. Don't have a copy of your business license or don't have one? How about a Yellow Pages ad in the phone book that's two years old? Do you have anything at all that can show that you've been working at the same job for at least two years? Lenders can get pretty creative, and so can your loan officer. But if you can't get past this test, then your choices will be severely limited to no document status or loans from a private investor.

Many times the issue regarding proving income is the result of being paid in cash. If your employer pays you in cash on a per-job basis, it's vital that you get your employer to provide you with a wage summary. A wage summary tells anyone who properly asks how much you get paid and how often. The problem with people who are paid in cash is that often they simply keep it, with no record of its receipt. If you are paid in cash and you want to buy a home, it's essential that you open up a bank account to deposit such receipts. When you make those cash deposits, your lender will be able to match what your employer says you are being paid with what you put into your bank account. You can provide your W2s from the previous two years to show your income, but you'll also need to document your year-to-date earnings. For people who get paid by check, the employer usually enters the year-to-date earnings on the check summary. If you get paid in cash, your employer will need to complete a

Verification of Employment form that is provided by your loan officer. It's here that your employer will state how much you make and how much money you've made so far this year.

If this is still a problem, your loan choices will be limited to no documentation, no income, or no income, no asset.

Loan Fraud

Engaging in loan fraud is tempting, especially with loans that require very little or no documentation. However, loan fraud is bad news. It doesn't just lead to a slap on the wrist; people go to prison for it.

And it's not small potatoes. With the advent of the Internet, AUSs, identity theft, and each subsequent technological advance in mortgage lending, good old-fashioned crime finds new ways to get to the table.

There are plenty of ways to commit loan fraud on an application, and they all involve the same thing—lying. The most common lie may be about income. In cases of mortgage fraud, it's usually the borrower who makes arrangements with others to help pull the wool over the lender's eyes.

Let's say a borrower has paid his rent more than 30 days past his due date nearly every month for a year. Knowing that getting approved with such a lousy rental history will be tough, he makes arrangements with a friend to pose as his landlord. The lender then sends the "landlord" a form asking how much the borrower's rent is and if the borrower has ever been late with his rent. If he was late, then how late was he?

Or the borrower fakes her income by changing some information on her paycheck stub or makes a fake W2. How does a lender combat such fraud?

Lenders have been around the block a few times. And no, the borrower just mentioned didn't invent a new way to get around a bad rental history. Several years ago, a lender would accept a rental verification form from an individual just as easily as it would accept a mortgage rating from a credit report. Not anymore. Lenders now want something a little more than someone's verbal or written verification.

Why? Well, let's say it's tempting to fudge a little when your credit history is less than stellar. A lender will now ask for 12 months' cancelled checks. Not 12 months' worth of checks made out to the fictitious landlord, but the front and the back of those checks, showing a cancellation date.

What, no cancelled checks? The borrower paid with a money order? Fine; let's see the copies of the money orders. All 12 of them. I'm sorry, no copies? You sometimes paid with cash? Then we're sorry, too. No loan approval.

It's also not too much of a stretch to imagine a real landlord giving out a sterling rental history verification when the renter was anything but sterling. Why would a landlord do such a thing? To get that no-good deadbeat renter out of his rental house, that's why. No, a lender wants to get just a little more than warm fuzzies when approving a loan.

Did the borrower provide a fake pay stub? Lenders can verify employment and payment history by making a phone call to the employer. There are even businesses that specialize in employment verification that the lender can call. Lenders can also get copies of previously filed tax returns when the borrower gives them IRS form 4506, asked for on almost every loan application.

Lenders get real serious when it comes to fraudulent loans. People go to jail, plain and simple.

There are advertisements that promise to erase all your bad credit legally by having you simply "start all over" with a new identity. Sounds easy enough, right? But it's against the law. It also goes against the mortgage application, which asks, "Have you ever been known by any other name?" If you say no, then you just lied on your application.

Loan fraud has actually been made easier by the lenders themselves with the advent of low and no documentation loans, where applicants cross their hearts and hope to die that what they put on the mortgage application is true. Buying a house, moving in, and being paranoid that every time there's a knock at the door, it's the FBI isn't worth it. There are so many loan options available that loan fraud simply isn't worth it. If the loan is properly structured, almost anyone can get a mortgage.

CHAPTER 8

Buying with No Money Down

There are as many reasons to buy with no money down as there are people on the planet. Or at least, there could be. Buying without putting any money into the equation means that you're leveraging as much as you possibly can. When you make no down payment, you're borrowing 100 percent of the value of the home. But why would anyone do such a thing? Doesn't everyone put at least something down when buying real estate?

It used to be that, yes, almost everyone put something down. The only loan program that required zero down payment was a Veterans Administration loan, or VA loan, which we'll discuss in the next chapter.

When lenders make loans, they look at all the variables such as:

Sufficient income. This means the ability to make monthly payments on time. The borrower has enough money not just to make the house payment, but also to eat, buy clothes, pay taxes, or whatever else he needs money for. Lenders like to make loans, but they don't like to foreclose.

Credit history. Not only is the borrower *able* to pay the loan back, but she is also *willing* to pay back the loan on time. This is the credit history. How and when a borrower repays her debts can determine the outcome of a mortgage loan.

Down payment. Most loans have the lender saying something like, "Okay, we'll loan you some money, but we want to see a little 'blood, sweat, and tears' from you, if that's okay." The blood, sweat, and tears takes the form of hard-earned cash—your down payment money. A lender will relax some lending guidelines if the borrower puts more money down.

But making a down payment isn't as much of a requirement any longer. There are more and more loan programs available that don't require any money down whatsoever. This is a huge change over the past few years that few consumers know about. Many consumers think that no-money-down loans are some type of card-shuffle game where the entire transaction may not be on the up-and-up, or that there's some hidden "catch" when it comes to no-money-down programs. That's not the case.

Different people might have different motivations for choosing a no-money-down avenue, but users of most zero down payment programs are motivated by not having any money in the bank or having money in the bank but not wanting to use it.

No Money in the Bank

This may seem a little too obvious, but in fact it may be the most common and simplest reason: There are no cookies in the cookie jar. And no matter how hard the buyers try, there are no cookies left at the end of the month. Everything's gone, and they're living paycheck to paycheck.

This is all too common. In housing markets where home prices appreciate month after month, two things generally happen: Housing demand increases, and property taxes increase because of the increased valuation of property. For rental housing, that means that the landlord both can and must raise the rent: *Can* because the market forces permit it, and *must* because the costs to the landlord, in the form of higher taxes, have increased.

There was a couple that got married and rented their first apartment together. Each time their lease came up for renewal, they saw a rent increase. And they had done nothing more than live in the apartment and pay their rent on time. They tried to save, but they could come up with little at the end of each month. In fact, because of low interest rates, they found that their rent payments were actually higher than a mortgage payment would be.

Then they had their first child. Then their second. They needed a bigger apartment or rental house, but again the rent was higher than a house payment. The more they tried to save, "life" happened to them in the form of a family, higher rents, and everything that goes along with these things. They were stuck.

Unfortunately, they were stuck when they didn't need to be. They thought, like most people, that in order to buy a house, they needed a down payment. Not only that, but many people also think that 20 percent or more is needed before a lender will even talk to a borrower. Not true.

I showed them several no-money-down loans, and they're now happy homeowners. But they didn't have to wait as long as they did. They could have bought a few years ago.

Don't Want to Use the Money in the Bank

In this situation, it's simply a matter of choice. Yes, there's money in the bank, but no, I'm not going to use it to buy a home. Some people, in fact, might want to put less money down to buy a home and instead use that money to invest in other things.

For instance, there's a home for sale at $200,000. A 20 percent down payment would amount to $40,000. Automatically, the buyers have a $40,000 equity position in the home. Automatically, their bank account is nearly empty. No longer are they "liquid"; their $40,000 is now in the form of wood, bricks, and carpet.

But the buyers don't want to put any money down. Instead, they take that money and invest it in the stock market. If they put no money down and their home increases in value by 5 percent per year, and if they invest their $40,000 and get a 6 percent return each year, after 10 years they have:

$110,000 in equity gain from their house by paying the mortgage payments

$33,000 in earnings from investments

Some people may have the money to put down but simply choose not to do so. It's a choice, not a necessity.

Money's Available, but Not Right Now

This is common when people own a piece of property but can't put anything down on another property until they sell the one they already own. Usually this happens when someone has his own property listed but hasn't gotten any takers.

You'll see this happen in areas where the market is super-hot and properties don't take very long to sell. Or when a prospective buyer's perfect "dream home" comes on the market, but she doesn't have any down payment money. She'd like to buy the new home, but she figures she can't because the down payment funds are tied up in her existing home.

Or the buyer has other investments that have value, but he can't get to them fast enough or cheaply enough, such as retirement funds like 401(k) or IRA accounts. In this instance, there's money available; it's just tied up.

Properties Are Appreciating

What better way to leverage than with zero down? None that I know of. If you're in an area where home prices are continuing to increase, then buying with no money down takes full advantage of leveraging your assets.

As property values increase, so does your equity. Compare that to another type of investment, such as a share of company stock. You can't buy the share for zero dollars, right? No, you had to pay something for it. Then you sit back and (hopefully) the value of your share increases.

But with zero down, you've done one better: You've watched the value of your asset increase without putting in any money of your own whatsoever.

Let's look at a home valued at $400,000, and suppose that home prices in the area have increased by 15 percent in each of the previous three years and your Realtor indicates that similar increases can be expected over the next three years.

You do some homework, and you discover that new homes are being built at a rapid rate, existing homes are selling fast, and new businesses are transferring to your area. What's more, Dell has decided to open up a brand-new manufacturing plant, hiring an additional three thousand employees. Looks like it might be a good time to buy, right?

If you bought a $400,000 home and prices appreciated by 15 percent each year, after three years your home would be worth around $600,000. You put nothing down, and you now have $200,000 in equity. You can sell the home, get a home equity line of credit (HELOC) to tap into the equity without selling, or simply do nothing and watch your home increase in value.

On the other hand, homes can decrease in value, just as they can increase. You're always taking a risk when you look at any real estate as an investment. Sometimes the risk pays off; sometimes it costs.

Reasons *Not* to Buy with No Money Down

Even when no-money-down opportunities are available, there are times when they should be given a little more scrutiny. Here are some reasons *not* to buy with no money down.

You may plan on moving within a couple of years. Let's face it, buying or selling a home costs money. You'll see that on every closing statement. The Realtor gets paid, the lender gets paid, the insurance person gets paid, and on and on. When you sell a property, you can also expect to pay. You'll pay the Realtor, more title insurance, closing fees, and more. For a home with a $150,000 sales price, closing costs of $12,000 or more are not uncommon.

When you buy with no money down, that of course means that you have no initial equity; the only equity you can gain is from natural market appreciation.

For example, suppose you buy a home for $150,000 with an annual appreciation rate of 10 percent. One year later, your home is worth $150,000 plus $15,000, or $165,000. Note that 10 percent is a fairly hefty rate, although, as many people saw in the early to mid-2000s, it is hardly uncommon. Still, such appreciation rates are the exception and not the rule.

If the appreciation rate is 20 percent, then after one year your home will be worth $150,000 plus $30,000, or $180,000. You will then have $30,000 in equity as a result of nothing more than a "hot" market. But what if you're not in a hot market? What if you're in a normal market? What if homes appreciate by 5 percent? Or 3 percent? Even worse, what if there is no appreciation whatsoever?

And you could be lucky to have no appreciation. In certain areas, home values can decline from one year to the next. In a town where the big industry is making pillowcases, suppose that the owner of the factory decides to make pillowcases in a far-away country. All the jobs go overseas, and a lot of townsfolk are put out of work. These people can't find work in that town, and they soon find that they can't pay their bills, either. They have to move. So they sell their home.

Because there are too many sellers and not enough buyers, homes actually decrease in price. It's a sad story, but all too often a true one.

Using the same $150,000 sales price and $12,000 in closing costs, here is what would happen using different appreciation rates.

20% appreciation	$30,000	Less costs $12,000	Net to seller $18,000
15% appreciation	$22,500	Less costs $12,000	Net to seller $10,500
10% appreciation	$15,000	Less costs $12,000	Net to seller $3,000
5% appreciation	$7,500	Less costs $12,000	Loss to seller $4,500
o appreciation	$0	Less costs $12,000	Loss to seller $12,000
5% depreciation	−$7,500	Less costs $12,000	Loss to seller $19,500

When property values continually increase, everybody's happy. (At least, everybody except perhaps current buyers.) But when properties don't increase or, worse, decrease, then the seller has no equity with which to pay the closing costs. This is sometimes called "bringing a check to the closing table," as the seller must dip into her own funds to make the deal work.

Closing costs have to be considered when buying a home. If your property doesn't appreciate enough to cover potential settlement charges, putting no money down places you at risk of having to bring a check to the closing table. Yuck.

Another reason someone may not want to buy with no money down has to do with depreciation. Usually any given market is either a "seller's market" or a "buyer's market." This means that in times of moderate to heavy home demand, the sellers can set the price of a home. When you see bidding wars taking place in a home market, then it's a seller's market. In a buyer's market, it's the buyers who control both the pace of sales and the price of homes. This means slower selling times and lower home prices. How do you know if a particular market is hot or cold? You can do all the research you want, but the easiest way is to use a Realtor when buying or selling.

In a soft market, where home prices are fading, it's not a good idea to go in with no money down. If home prices depreciate by 15 percent per year, then over the course of just a few short years (say three or four years), your $150,000 home will be worth only about $95,000. Ouch. Forget the hassles about closing costs. You're already "upside down" by $55,000. Just getting positive on the equity side could take years. And you still owe the lender nearly $150,000.

Now compare that same scenario with one in which you make a $30,000 down payment (20 percent). After that same three to four years, while your equity has disappeared, at least your obligation to the bank is just under $120,000 instead of $150,000.

Putting zero money down in a declining market can be a bad move. Consider such a scenario only if you plan on keeping the property long enough to recover both closing costs and equity lost because of market conditions.

CHAPTER 9

Government Programs with Zero Money Down

Your government—federal, state, and local—has programs designed to get you into a home without any down payment money. And while starting out with government loans might sound obvious, all too often people who are eligible for such programs either don't apply because they don't think they qualify or don't apply because they aren't aware of these programs.

Federal government programs include those backed by the Department of Veterans Affairs, or VA loans, those guaranteed by the Federal Housing Administration, or FHA, and the U.S. Department of Agriculture, or USDA.

Still further down the government food chain are county or city programs designed to help people come up with their down payment funds, either in the form of outright grants or as loans issued to cover down payments.

VA Loan Programs

Many moons ago, say in 1944, the federal government did a very good thing. As a reward for their service to the country, it gave qualified veterans lots of new benefits. One of those benefits was being able to buy a home without any money down.

Back then, no-money-down loans were few and far between. Down payments on certain loans would vary depending primarily on regional factors, such as which bank was the biggest or which savings and loan was making home loans. Down payment amounts of up to 50 percent of the sales price were not uncommon. Imagine that: Half down and the home is yours.

But the Veterans Administration came up with a stellar plan to thank qualified veterans and active-duty personnel through housing assistance. The VA doesn't actually make a VA loan, a lender does so, but if the loan goes into default, the VA will repay the loss to the lender. The VA guarantees the mortgage instead of issuing it.

Qualified Veterans

People who qualify for VA home benefits are:

Veterans

Active-duty personnel

Reserve troops with qualifying service

Surviving spouses of servicemen or women who have died in combat

For some reason, maybe because they are in fact a government product, VA loans can be complicated. There are many more government forms that the borrower must complete, and the loans are underwritten in a slightly different manner. That's why some facets of VA loans are often misunderstood. Here are some of those confusing areas:

The VA guarantees the loan, so any vet can qualify. No. The VA has credit standards, just like almost any other loan program. Just because a veteran has VA benefits doesn't mean that he can get a mortgage loan regardless of his credit status.

If a qualifying veteran has a recent bankruptcy, a foreclosure, or a recent history of late payments, then the lender isn't going to make the loan, regardless of any guarantee. There's an all-too-common misperception that a VA guarantee is a guarantee to the veteran. It's not. It's a guarantee to the lender that if the lender approves the loan using VA guidelines and the loan goes into default, the VA will reimburse the lender for any losses.

The VA benefit is good only once. No. The VA home loan benefit can be used over and over; it just can't be used more than once at the same time. In other words, a veteran can't use his VA benefit to buy one home, then use that same benefit to buy another while keeping the original loan. If a veteran uses her VA benefit to buy a home and wants to use it to buy another one, then she needs to retire the original home loan either by selling the home or by refinancing the loan with a conventional loan.

VA loans are good only for existing homes. No. VA loans can be used for new or existing homes, but the confusion arises from what is considered "new." While the VA will guarantee a construction loan, you won't find any lenders who will make a zero-money-down VA construction loan. Instead, the veteran must find a new home, have a home built by the builder with the builder's funds, or use an independent construction loan. At the end of construction, the veteran can use the VA loan to buy the new house.

Types of VA Loans

VA loans come in two types, much like any other loan program: fixed and adjustable hybrid. It's up to you and your loan officer to decide which is best, but generally you have two choices.

Choose a fixed rate if you anticipate being in the home for several years. Choose a hybrid if you're planning on owning the home for a shorter period of time. It's really that simple.

One of the features of VA loans is that the closing costs that veterans are allowed to pay are limited—a benefit that other conventional or government loans don't have. There are lots of closing costs involved when obtaining a mortgage, as listed in Chapter 24. But veterans get to pay less.

Veterans are allowed to pay only for appraisals, credit reports, title and title-related charges, origination fees and discount points, recording fees, and a survey where required. Everything else must be either absorbed by the lender or paid for by the seller. An easy way to remember which fees veterans are allowed to pay is to remember the acronym ACTORS: Appraisal, Credit, Title, Origination, Recording, and Survey.

There is also one other fee that the veteran must pay, but this fee can be rolled into the loan amount. It's called the funding fee, and it's equal to 2.0 percent of the loan amount. This fee is waived for veterans who receive service-connected disability.

Let's take a home that's for sale at $300,000. A qualifying veteran wants to buy that home and put no money down. With the funding fee of 2 percent included, the loan amount becomes $306,000.

There are in fact closing costs, although limited, that the veteran pays, or at least *may* pay. Let's look at the typical closing costs on a $300,000 VA loan:

Appraisal	$ 350
Credit report	$ 20
Title insurance	$ 500
Escrow	$ 150
Origination	$ 3,000
Recording	$ 100
Survey	$ 300

That adds up to $4,420. That's a lot of money. So instead of a zero-money-down VA loan, it becomes a zero-money-down VA loan with closing costs. A true zero-money-down home loan has no closing costs. Nothing. So what's a veteran to do? Have the seller pay these costs. Easier said than done, right? Not really. If the deal is structured properly, a seller on a VA loan (or any other loan, for that matter) can be persuaded to pay the buyer's closing costs.

First, as part of your offer to buy, ask the seller to pay your closing costs. There's no harm in asking, right? If the seller says no, simply increase the sales price by an amount equal to the closing costs, then again ask the seller to pay your costs. Why not, right? The seller gets what he originally asked for in terms of net proceeds from the sale, and you had your closing costs paid at the same time.

Yeah, I know, the loan amount also increased by the amount of the closing costs, but the difference in monthly payments is small compared to the outlay of funds in the form of closing fees. For example, on a $300,000 loan with $4,000 in veteran's closing fees and a 30-year fixed rate of 6 percent, the monthly principal and interest payment would be about $1,798. Plus you're out about $4,000 for the closing costs. Now increase the sales price to $304,000 and have the seller pay your fees. You keep the $4,000, and your payment goes up by only $24 a month. Not a bad trade-off.

Assumable VA loans

Assumable means that an owner can simply sign over the house and have the buyer (the assumer) take over the original mortgage along with ownership of the house. That's a great deal. Instead of applying for a loan, gathering all your paperwork, and going through the sometimes grueling process of getting a loan approval, all you need to do is assume the original VA loan.

There are two types of assumable mortgages: qualifying and non-qualifying.

Qualifying Assumable Mortgages

Qualifying assumables are loans that say that, yes, any borrower can assume the original note, but the borrower has to qualify just as if she were applying for a new mortgage. Her credit report will be checked, along with her rental or mortgage history and her employment history. Why would someone want to assume a qualifying mortgage when she could go out and get a brand new one?

When someone assumes a mortgage, she assumes everything about the original note. That means that whatever interest rate was on the original mortgage is the interest rate the new borrower will get. If interest rates were 5 percent when the original mortgage was issued and have gone up to 8 percent, then it makes sense to assume the old note.

Nonqualifying Assumable Mortgages

Nonqualifying assumables are loans that anyone can assume, regardless of past credit history, income level, or payment patterns. This is sometimes called a VA No-Qual loan. Anyone can assume the note.

In 1988, the VA got rid of the nonqualifying assumption and replaced it with a qualified standard. This saved the VA lots of money. Allowing people who had bad credit or had no intention of paying back the loan to assume VA loans meant that VA lenders had to foreclose on a lot of properties, and because of the VA guarantee, the VA had to fork over a bunch of money.

VA assumables are a way to get into a no money down VA loan, but that doesn't mean that the person selling the home to you won't want any money from you. Let's say that a veteran used her VA eligibility to buy a home and paid $250,000 for it. Five years later, she decides to sell the home and offer the VA assumable note along with it.

But home prices have increased during that time, and now the home is worth $290,000. Yes, the VA note is assumable, and, yes, you can assume it, but the veteran wants another $40,000. You have to come up with that difference or find some other form of financing. What originally was a zero-money-down loan for the veteran now means you can assume it if you come up with the difference between $250,000 and $290,000. That's hardly a zero-money-down loan, is it?

Fifteen or twenty years ago, VA assumables were a great way for people who had credit or down payment issues to buy a home. The original VA loans were nonqualified assumables issued to qualified veterans. Now, however, finding a nonqualified assumable loan is nearly impossible—especially without a considerable amount of down payment from the new borrower.

FHA Loan Programs

In 1934, the Federal Housing Administration, or FHA, was formed to foster home ownership. The country was still in the Depression, so the federal government embarked on a series of efforts to help get the country's economy moving. One of the expected benefits of helping people buy homes was that the homeowners would also buy other things. Purchases of couches, beds, pillows, drapes, paint, and other such housing-related items would spur the economy and make everyone happy homeowners.

The FHA used a guarantee similar to that of the VA. If an FHA loan went bad, the government would pay back the lender. Just like the VA, the FHA doesn't make the loan; it simply guarantees the loan as long as the lender issuing it followed FHA guidelines.

While FHA loans aren't actually zero money down, they are nearly so. The FHA borrower needs to have only 3 percent in a purchase transaction. Note that I said "needs to have in a transaction," not "down payment." There are closing costs, insurance policies, and the FHA's version of a VA funding fee, called the mortgage insurance premium (MIP), as well as a down payment.

Instead of trying to calculate a 3 percent down payment plus closing fees plus seller-paid costs plus MIP, the FHA simply requires a 3 percent minimum investment by the borrower. If a home sells for $200,000, then the buyer is required to come to the closing table with at least 3 percent of that amount, or $6,000. That $6,000 can be applied to any part of the buyer's liability in the purchase, but at the end of the closing, the buyer has still put only 3 percent into the deal.

And just as a buyer using a VA loan can have the seller pay closing costs, a seller in an FHA transaction can pay the buyer's closing fees in a similar fashion. The FHA also limits the closing costs that a borrower can pay, meaning that other "nonallowables" must be paid by the lender or the seller. Allowable closing costs for an FHA borrower include the following:

Appraisal and inspection charges
Credit report fees
Points and origination charges
All title and title-related work
Document preparation charges
Attorney and settlement fees

That might sound like the gamut of closing costs, but most nonallowable charges come from the lender and can include such things as application charges, processing fees, administration fees, or other lender "junk" charges. If you want a no-closing-cost FHA loan, you can negotiate the sales price of the home to accommodate the additional closing costs.

There are no income limits for an FHA loan, you don't have to be a first-time home buyer to get one, and there are no other special qualifying characteristics of FHA loans. This is a government-sponsored program that is available to anyone who can qualify under ordinary income and credit guidelines.

Zero-Money-Down FHA Loans

Even though the FHA does require the borrower to put 3 percent into the transaction, it makes certain allowances not available on other loans that directly affect the amount of funds needed by the buyer to close a sale. One of the most important features of an FHA loan is the allowance for a "gift" to be made to the buyer. FHA permits gifts to cover the down payment and closing fees as long as the gift comes from one of the following:

A family member

The borrower's employer

A labor union of which the borrower is a member

A government agency designed to assist homeowners

A nonprofit organization established for down payment assistance

For instance, if you're one of the lucky people who have a family member willing to help buy you a home, the FHA allows a family member to flat-out give you the money for your 3 percent required investment. That's a zero-money-down loan program. Your employer can help; if you're a union member, your union can help; and other agencies established to help people buy homes can help.

Yet another advantage of an FHA loan is the allowance for grants, gifts, and loans to be issued by others to help close the deal. These can come from organizations established to help people come up with their down payment and closing cost money. Few people are aware of the ability of FHA borrowers to find funds that can help offset their 3 percent requirement.

What a deal, right? You find a home, but you don't have any money to put down or pay for closing costs. Then, right out of the blue, an organization comes along and says, "Guess what? We'll give you the money to buy a home!" You've never heard of such organizations? You're not alone, but they're out there. Depending upon where you live, you can research the names and addresses of enterprises that do just that—give you money. These enterprises are discussed later in this chapter.

USDA and Rural Housing Service

The Rural Housing Service, or RHS, formerly known as the Farmers Home Administration (FmHA), Zero Down Loans is still another government program, not to be confused with the FHA. The FmHA program is now a part of the U.S. Department of Agriculture, or USDA, which has as part of its overall government goal to provide rural homes to those who qualify and who have not been able to be approved elsewhere. (The FmHA acronym is still used by most people, but in fact it is now the RHS.)

The target for this program is rural communities, not urban ones, with a population that does not exceed 10,000. There are no down payments and no mortgage insurance required, and the loan can go up to 102 percent of the value of the home, allowing the borrower to roll some or all of the closing costs into the loan.

There are no income limits, loan limits, or other limitations with this loan program, which is geared toward promoting rural development and home ownership in rural communities. The program, while not requiring mortgage insurance, allows the borrower to choose to put $2,000 of his own money into the transaction. The difference in the final monthly payment would be maybe about ten bucks or so a month, depending upon the sales price of the home.

This is a little-known government program and perhaps one of the easiest loans to get approved for. The drawback is that these loans are property- and area-specific—you won't find them in downtown Dallas, for example. However, you might find them available 60 miles west of there. For more information on USDA home loans, visit www.rurdev .usda.gov.

Down Payment Assistance Programs

Down payment assistance programs, or DPAPs, come in two flavors: grants and loans. While these grants and loans don't necessarily come from government agencies, many of them do, and if they don't, they generally come from nonprofit or 501(c)(3) organizations.

Grants from nonprofits are the easiest. Such a grant is nothing more than a gift to you to enable you to buy the home. You don't have to pay it back. There are several variations on this theme, but the most common form is that the seller makes a donation to the nonprofit DPAP, and the DPAP then makes a donation to the buyer equal to the amount the seller donated. The nonprofit is set up as a legal charity under federal tax statutes. The nonprofit covers its overhead by deducting a small administration fee from the donation, usually about three or four hundred bucks.

Let's say the house you want to buy costs $200,000 and you need $8,000 to close the deal, which includes a 3 percent down payment of $6,000 plus closing costs of $2,000. The seller of the home makes a donation of $8,000 to the nonprofit, which in turn sends that $8,000 to the closing table. Okay, it won't be exactly $8,000, as the nonprofit group will deduct the transaction fee, but that fee is minor. You're getting your down payment plus closing costs covered for free, with no strings attached. I'm not kidding.

You need to be careful and get your ducks in a row before moving forward. First, you'll need to secure a mortgage that allows gift funds from a nonprofit as part or all of your down payment, such as an FHA loan, a Community Homebuyer loan from Fannie Mae, or a Neighborhood Advantage loan from Freddie Mac. (These loans are discussed in the next chapter.) The fact that you're getting a grant to help you buy the home doesn't mean that you don't have to qualify for the mortgage. You still have to qualify for the mortgage first and foremost, or nothing happens.

Second, you'll need to find a nonprofit organization that participates in DPAPs. There is a list of available institutions in Appendix C at the back of this book. Third, you'll need to find a Realtor that participates in these programs and a lender that knows what's going on with them. It may take a little homework on your part, so it's best to find someone who has worked with these organizations before.

Grants are available in nearly every town and city, but their usage levels aren't what they could be. This isn't because there aren't any institutions out there that are willing to help people. Yet these grants are still sometimes hard to find. Why?

Loan officers don't know about them, and since they're different, loan officers may not want to mess with them. Your best bet might be to find a loan officer who deals primarily in FHA loans. Another reason DPAPs are hard to find is that most of their money goes toward their overhead, so there's not much left for advertising.

Your Realtor needs to know about these programs as well. And did I mention the seller? Here's the key element: The seller is going to have to be willing to make, in this example, an $8,000 donation. Why would the seller want to do that?

Most wouldn't unless they are having some problems selling the property. Slow markets can motivate sellers. Your Realtor should know if such a transaction will work in your market. Or, guess what else? Simply increase the sales price to accommodate the donation. As long as the sales price is supported by an appraisal, this should help convince a seller to help you buy the home. An appraisal is the determining factor supporting market value, and if the home can sell in an open market for

$208,000 and there are comparable sales in the area to support that value, then you're home free.

Some DPAPs offer loans, some that you have to pay back and some that you don't. Some have income requirements (meaning that your income can't exceed a certain amount), while still others require you to take a home ownership class.

CHAPTER 10

Conventional Zero-Down Loan Programs

Conventional in this sense means a home loan issued by a mortgage lender that is backed by the lender itself and not guaranteed by the government as VA and FHA loans are. Conventional mortgage financing is much like government loans in that these loans must be underwritten to meet universal guidelines. Most conventional underwriting is written to Federal National Mortgage Association (FNMA or Fannie Mae) and Federal Home Loan Mortgage Corporation (FHLMC or Freddie Mac) standards.

In the early part of the last century, only the fortunate could afford home ownership. In 1938, as part of the newly formed FHA, Fannie Mae was created to help provide liquidity in the mortgage marketplace.

Liquidity is important because lenders, by their nature, make money by lending it out. When they run out of money to lend, they can only collect the monthly interest payments. While that's fine, if an opportunity that the lender wanted to invest in were to arise, well, the lender couldn't do it. A lender might have assets of $100 million, but it wasn't exactly in the lender's bank vaults—it was tied up in people's houses.

Fannie Mae's mission was, and still is, to foster home ownership. It does this by buying mortgage loans from lenders. As long as a mortgage loan was issued under Fannie Mae's guidelines, that loan can be bought and sold, not just by Fannie Mae, but also by other investors who make money by buying mortgages from other lenders.

Along with liquidity, the Fannie Mae standards help the mortgage market keep a type of conformity. Lots of money can change hands, but if the mortgages are exactly alike, with only the borrowers and the property being different, then lenders are in fact trading a commodity. Buying and selling a universal commodity helps keeps rates low. The more there is of a certain product, the cheaper it will get.

Fannie Mae and Freddie Mac are government-sponsored enterprises, or GSEs. Nice work if you can get it. They were commissioned by the federal government to foster homeownership, and they are still backed by the U.S. government. However, you can also invest in them because their stock is publicly traded. They're "quasi-governmental" agencies in that their stock is public, yet they're government-chartered.

Having your stock traded publicly means that you owe your loyalty to your stockholders. And like the CEO of any corporation, the CEOs of these companies' main job is to make their shareholders more money. Fannie Mae and Freddie Mac have been, give or take, doing just that over the years.

But in addition to making more money on traditional types of loans, the CEOs also need to think up ways to make new types of loans, therefore making more money—they hope. For years, conventional loans from Fannie Mae and Freddie Mac required 20 percent down. Period. That kept a lot of people out of homes because it took so much time to save the down payment. Then, about 50 years ago, a company called Mortgage Guaranty Insurance Company, or MGIC, came up with an idea that changed the way conventional mortgages were made.

MGIC provided an insurance policy, paid by the borrowers in favor of the lender, that allowed the borrower to put less than 20 percent down—say 5 percent. The remaining 15 percent would be "insured" by MGIC in case of borrower default. I'll give you an example.

A home is listed for $200,000. Historically, a conventional mortgage would require 20 percent down, or $40,000. But the buyers didn't have $40,000; they had only $10,000, or 5 percent. Instead of waiting several more years and saving up the money, the borrowers bought an insurance policy from MGIC for the difference between the standard 20 percent down and their own 5 percent down. In this case, the policy was for $30,000. If the borrowers defaulted on the note, then MGIC would owe the original lender the $30,000 difference. That meant that a borrower would be underwritten first by the lender, then also by the insurance company, using similar underwriting guidelines.

Mortgage insurance rates can vary by loan type and amount down, but a good rule of thumb is about $1/2$ percent of the loan amount, divided by 12 to get the monthly mortgage insurance premium. In this case, $1/2$ percent of $200,000 is $1,000. Divide that by 12 and the borrower would pay $83 per month for mortgage insurance. The borrower pays the premium, but the lender gets the benefit if the borrower defaults.

After several years, Fannie Mae and Freddie Mac decided that they wanted to add a few more loan programs to their mortgage mix. In addition to 30-year fixed-rate loans, they added 15-year and 20-year programs. Then they added adjustable-rate mortgages. Then hybrids. Then balloons. Then all sorts of loan programs designed to make more loans to more people so that they could make more money to give to their shareholders. Then they invented the zero-down mortgage.

Freddie Mac and Fannie Mae Zero-Down Loans

The name is straightforward. No longer do Fannie Mae and Freddie Mac require a down payment on all of their loans. While they used to accept as little as 5 percent, then even as low as 3 percent, in recent years they have introduced zero-down loan programs.

Not everyone knows about them, primarily because they're not advertised or marketed aggressively. Some people don't know about them because their loan officer at the bank didn't know about them—but they're there.

These loan programs may be called Community Homebuyer programs or Affordable Housing programs or other such names. In fact, lenders may package a zero-money-down loan program and call it anything they want. As long as they approve the loan using Fannie Mae or Freddie Mac's guidelines, they're okay.

Freddie Mac has a program it calls "HomePossible 100" that allows for no down payment by the borrower. Fannie Mae has a similar program that it calls "My Community Mortgage." Okay, these mortgages aren't exactly zero down. The borrower must have $500 in the transaction somewhere. That $500 will probably go toward closing costs. These zero-down loan programs have special income requirements that the borrowers must meet; specifically, the borrower's income may not exceed the median income for the area.

This program also has relaxed credit and debt ratio guidelines, again as long as the consumer meets the qualifications.

The HomePossible 100 program is not just zero down, but allows the borrower to also borrow his closing costs—up to 105 percent of the value of the home. Here the borrower puts zero down, and also borrows all of his closing costs along with the purchase price. Remember, the borrower must provide $500 somewhere in the transaction, but here's an example of a HomePossible 100 structure.

Sales price	$ 150,000
Down payment	$ 0
Closing costs	$ 3,000
Loan Amount	$ 152,500

In this case, the home sold for $150,000 and the closing costs totaled $3,000. Subtract the required $500 minimum investment from the buyer and the total loan amount was $152,500.

With a 30-year fixed rate of 7.5 percent, the monthly principal and interest payment works out to $1,066. But wait; recall that with any conventional mortgage with less than 20 percent down, mortgage insurance is required. And as with other insurance policies, the greater the risk, the higher the premium, right? A mortgage with no down payment is riskier for the lender than one with 10 percent down. That means that the mortgage insurance premium is higher. With 10 percent down, the monthly mortgage insurance premium would be about $45 on a $150,000 note.

With 5 percent down, the premium goes to $63, and with zero money down, the monthly mortgage insurance payment jumps to $127.

There's a higher monthly premium for zero down, yes. But it's a lot less than coming up with another $7,500 at closing for a 5 percent down loan.

Freddie also has another loan program that's similar to the Home-Possible 100 but doesn't have any income limitations. It's simply called the Freddie 100, and lenders have named it pretty much anything they want. The difference between this product and the HomePossible 100 is that there are no income limitations, it is not designed for the first-time buyer, and the credit requirements are a little tougher; however, they are no more stringent than for other conventional mortgage loans with down payments involved.

Fannie Mae has an offering called the "Flexible 100," which mostly follows the same guidelines as Freddie Mac's program.

All that is required for the Freddie 100 program is to get an Accept or better from Freddie Mac's AUS. Another big difference between Freddie's two programs is that the rate on the Freddie 100 loan will be slightly better than that on the HomePossible 100. Fannie Mae also requires only an approval using its AUS and documenting the file using the AUS guidelines.

80/20 Financing

An 80/20 loan is so called because it's made up of two loans. It's sometimes called a *piggyback* because the smaller loan "piggybacks" on the first note. The first loan is for 80 percent of the sales price of the house, and the second mortgage is for 20 percent of the sales price. That means that there is no down payment, and it also means that no private mortgage insurance is required because the first mortgage is for 80 percent of the sales price. But there are some curves involved in these loans that you need to be aware of.

First, not every lender offers such a program, although most do. Some lenders will make both the first and the second mortgage, while others will issue only the first mortgage, and you have to find someone else to issue the second.

If a lender will issue only the first mortgage, you need to make sure that the lender won't have a problem with your getting a second mortgage for the entire remaining balance. Almost every lender offers a piggyback, but usually they're of the 80/15/5 nature, meaning that you put 5 percent down and get an 80 percent first mortgage and a 15 percent second mortgage, or an 80/10/10. But the lender has to know about the structure of your entire loan.

If you're getting a second mortgage, the lender will want to know the terms of the note and how much you're borrowing. Lenders need to know this information so that they can calculate your debt ratios accurately. If the lender doesn't know about your second payment, then how can it arrive at your true ratio?

Piggybacks with less down usually mean that the first lender will be a bit more strict in terms of underwriting. The lender has a bit more breathing room with an 80/10/10 than it does with an 80/15/5. And it has no breathing room whatsoever with an 80/20 because there is no cash down payment on your part.

How do these different programs compare? They're all mostly the same, the obvious difference being that your monthly payments are higher if you don't put anything down. Let's compare the differences using a $200,000 sales price.

100%		80/20		80/15/5	
Rate	7.50%	Rate	7.25%/10.00%	Rate	7.00%/8.00%
Payment	$1,565	Payment	$1,469	Payment	$1,284

Private mortgage insurance is included in the payment for the 100 percent mortgage

Without any down payment, the payments on the 100 percent mortgage and the 80/20 mortgage are within $100 of each other; depending upon whether lower rates are available by paying points, they'll generally be much the same. Finally, you can see that the payment for the 80/15/5 is a couple of hundred dollars less each month because of both the lower rate associated with a standard mortgage and borrowing less money by making a 5 percent down payment.

Silent Seconds

Silent seconds are second mortgages that no one except you and the person issuing the second mortgage is supposed to know about. Silent seconds aren't that uncommon. In fact, I sometimes hear people talk about them—Realtors, loan officers, and title people included—as though they were pretty much the rule of the road. They're not. They're silent for a reason: They're illegal.

What's so illegal about them? Lenders make loans based upon a lot of things, and two of the most important things are your debt ratios and your equity position, or down payment. Silent seconds affect both. If a lender issues you a mortgage loan for 80 percent of the value of the home, it's going to assume that you have a 20 percent down payment. That's one of the factors it takes into account in approving your loan. The lender also looks at your debt ratios with 20 percent down. If your ratios are at 45 percent, then your loan could be approved on those terms.

But enter the silent second. Suddenly you have zero equity, and because you're borrowing more money, your ratios could zoom into the stratosphere. The lender would never know—that is, until you couldn't afford the home any longer, so the lender foreclosed. And during your foreclosure proceedings, it finds out about the second mortgage you didn't mention.

Now your lender's attorneys contact the FBI because you committed loan fraud, and you have to go to jail for a while.

Silent seconds are usually carried by the seller of the property and are sometimes made by people who simply want the deal to close. This could be the borrower or the Realtor or anyone involved in the transaction, for that matter. The seller is told something like, "Hey, we're a little short on funds here; do you think you could carry a loan outside of the closing to carry our buyer over for a little while? No one has to know." Unfortunately, because silent seconds have become common in some areas, consumers may think they're not only common but also legal.

Unconventional Zero-Down Mortgage Loans from Lenders

So far, we've discussed loans that are guaranteed or offered through the federal government, such as the VA, FHA, and USDA, and also those from conventional sources that are underwritten to Fannie Mae and Freddie Mac standards. But for these loans, you typically need to have good credit. Not excellent in all cases, but still good.

In addition, all of the previous loan options are for primary residences only—you have to live there to get qualified. What about "unconventional" financing? Guess what? There are sources for those types of loans as well.

Unconventional financing is actually a loose term. While conventional lending means that it is a bank or mortgage lender that is responsible for approving and funding mortgage loans using Fannie or Freddie standards, *unconventional* means something other than who made the loan. An unconventional mortgage is made by a bank or mortgage lender, but it is made to guidelines other than the Fannie/Freddie mix. It's nothing really bad; it's just not . . . well, conventional.

Most 100 percent lending in this arena is done for a couple of reasons. One is that the purchase price of the property you're buying is above the loan limits set by Fannie Mae or Freddie Mac. The other reason these loans have a place in the market involves the qualification characteristics of the borrower.

These loans can accommodate various levels of documentation requirements that government and conventional loans cannot. If a borrower needs a stated income 100 percent loan, he won't find one under the conventional umbrella. Government and conventional 100 percent loans are for fully documented borrowers only. There's no room for stated anything. Unconventional 100 percent financing can fit a variety of borrower profiles.

Where do you find unconventional loans? At the same place you find every other loan: at your mortgage company. A lender doesn't have to be an unconventional lender in order to offer these products. Such loans are made every day by lenders that you'd recognize, as well as probably by a lot more that you wouldn't.

Be prepared to pay a bit more in rate for these loans, sometimes as much as 1 or 2 percent above a conventional offering. If you can get a 7.00 percent 30-year fixed-rate conventional loan, then the rate may be as high as 9.00 percent for a nonconventional loan.

It's because of this rate disparity that hybrids are often the loan program of choice for 100 percent buyers. A 5/1 hybrid might be found at 6.00 or 7.00 percent rather than the 9.00 percent charged for a fixed rate. Borrowers can find straight 100 percent financing as well as piggybacks of the 80/20 model. The difference would be which lender carries which program.

Zero-Down Investment Property Loans

Government loans don't allow for any purchases of investment property whatsoever. These loans require you to live in the home you're buying. While conventional financing for investment or rental properties is available, it will require a higher interest rate and a larger down payment. How much higher?

First, a minimum of 10 percent down is required for conventional investment loans. And if your down payment is less than 20 percent, then mortgage insurance is required. Not only is it required, but it's also more expensive for investment property. A mortgage insurance monthly payment for an owner-occupied 10 percent down loan for $100,000 would be about $25 less than the payment for a rental property.

If you're looking to purchase investment property with no money down, your choices are limited. There are good loan products, mind you, but very few lenders offer them. In fact, many lenders or brokers will tell you that zero-down investment loans are simply not available except from private or individual lenders. That's not the case. I've placed many a zero-down investment loan. It's just that the requirements and loan terms are a tad more stringent than those for conventional fare, and these loans are just plain hard to find.

Zero-down investment loans are typically of the piggyback variety, meaning that there are two loans. The first loan is for 80 percent of the sales price, thereby eliminating the need for mortgage insurance, and the remaining 20 percent takes the form of a second mortgage. The rate on the second mortgage is higher than that on the first, as in all piggy-backs, and the mortgages are almost always either fixed for 30 or 15 years or balloons in 15 years.

Because such loans are at the top of the food chain with regard to risk for the lender, you can expect much higher rates. If the 30-year fixed rate on a 100 percent owner-occupied property is 9.00 percent, then your rate on a non-owner-occupied property will be another $1/2$ percent higher. This is another reason why hybrids are by far the most common loan form for 100 percent investor loans.

Why do people use such loans? Most people who buy investment property with no money down at higher than market rates do so because they intend to sell the property soon. They're speculating. If an investor finds a piece of property that she thinks is a real bargain but doesn't have or want to use the cash to buy it, she leverages the purchase as high as she can.

The idea is that the property will appreciate in value long before the term of the initial hybrid is up, and she will make a few thousand dollars. I once financed an entire subdivision in this fashion. The homes were built in a college town and were designed as student housing. They were mostly sold to real estate investors who saw them as a real bargain.

An investor would buy one of these houses with nothing down and choose either a 3/1 or 5/1 ARM. After one year, during which the house was rented out for much more than the mortgage payments, the investor sold the property for $30,000 more than what he had paid for them. The investors saw a bargain, "borrowed" someone else's money for about a year, and walked away from the table with $30,000. Some of these inves-tors bought as many as five homes apiece using these programs.

Such loans are hard to qualify for. And why not? No money down for investment property? Lenders know that if borrowers ever get into fi-nancial straits, they'll let their rental properties be foreclosed upon before they'll give up their primary residence. Makes sense, right?

That's why lenders increase both the rate and the down payment requirement for real estate investors. Furthermore, they also increase other qualifying characteristics, such as the requirement for liquid assets.

Other programs might also require that the borrower have previous experience in owning investment properties, such as being able to not only make the mortgage payment on time but also take care of the maintenance and other tenant issues as they arise.

Zero-Down Loans for Bad Credit

Yes, there are loans available to those with bad credit that require no down payment. While conventional loans may not require a specific credit score or debt ratio requirement, loans designed for those with bad credit are very specific in their lending guidelines. But they do in fact exist and are offered by lenders whose names you would recognize. They're just not as common. And they rely heavily on credit scores. We'll explore credit scores in greater detail in Chapter 15, but scores can be much more important with no-money-down, bad-credit mortgages.

While zero-down loans for those with good credit look for a credit score of around 680, subprime zero-down loans will accept a score as low as 580. That spread of 100 points between a score of 580 and 680 usually requires an additional 1.50 to 2.00 percent in rate.

For example, someone with good credit might find a rate of 7.00 percent on a $300,000 loan. On a 30-year loan, that works out to a payment of $1,995. At 9.00 percent, that payment jumps to $2,413. Quite a difference.

In addition, bad-credit, zero-down loans normally offer 2/28 or 3/27 loan terms, meaning that after two or three years, the loan turns into an annual adjustable-rate mortgage. Such subprime ARM loans carry much higher rates than conventional ARMs do. While a standard ARM might have a 2.75 percent margin, a subprime ARM could have a margin of 6.50 percent or higher, where allowed by law.

People with damaged credit who fall into the subprime category will find that subprime lenders are stricter when it comes to credit scores. While Fannie Mae and Freddie Mac may not have credit score requirements for a particular loan program, subprime lenders use the credit score as their bedrock for loan approval.

If someone has a credit score of 560 and the desired loan program requires a credit score of 570, then the borrower will typically have to wait until she gets some more down payment money, borrow less, or improve her score. There is very little room for loan exceptions in subprime lending.

Instead of making an exception, the subprime lender will usually offer a "counter," in which the original loan is declined but another offer is made instead. For instance, someone with a 560 score might be declined for a loan program that requires 570, but the lender could offer as an alternative a loan program with a higher rate or requiring a higher down payment.

Let's look at an example of a subprime zero-down loan commonly found on the market today.

Minimum credit score	620
Minimum down payment	-0-
Maximum debt ratios	45
Loan type	3/27
Prepayment penalty	3 years
Document type	Full

For a zero-down loan, this loan program offers a hybrid fixed-rate mortgage for three years, then turns into an annual adjustable. Maximum debt ratios, including housing and all consumer loans, cannot exceed 45 percent of gross monthly income, and there is a prepayment penalty on the loan for the first three years.

Most often you'll find that when there are prepayment penalties, the prepayment penalty period lasts as long as the initial fixed period of a hybrid. A 2/28 loan, for example, would have a two-year prepayment period, while a 3/27 loan would have a three-year prepayment period. This loan type also asks for full documentation.

For a loan amount of $200,000 at 8.00 percent, the monthly payment would be $1,467.

Changing some of the loan parameters can change the nature of the loan as well. If, for instance, the borrower wanted to go stated doc instead of full doc, he might anticipate an increase in interest rate of $1/4$ percent.

Or maybe the prepayment penalty can be "bought out" in the form of points.

Still another loan program that offers a 2/28 hybrid while still allowing a 45 percent debt ratio will let someone borrow more money with zero down simply because the starting interest rate is $1/2$ percent lower than that on a 3/27. Follow all of that? It's difficult. That's why such loan programs have matrices that even their loan officers have trouble remembering.

There are no "typical" zero-down, bad-credit loans. Instead, you will literally see a loan matrix that combines all the various credit factors, such as score, ratios, and loan programs offered.

One interesting note about subprime zero-down loans is that when a conventional 30-year fixed-rate, no-money-down loan is compared with a subprime hybrid, the monthly payments are remarkably similar.

Let's compare a $250,000 zero-down loan using a conventional 30-year fixed-rate product offered by a mortgage company at 7.00 percent with a subprime 3/27 hybrid offered to a borrower with a credit score of 680. A typical spread between those two loan types is about $1/2$ percent, or, in this example a rate of 7.50 percent for the subprime mortgage.

30-year fixed-rate conventional	$1,663
3/27 subprime hybrid	$1,748

Not much of a difference is there? Granted, we're not really comparing apples to apples with a 30-year fixed and a hybrid ARM, but this gives us an intriguing twist—especially when we add the cost of mortgage insurance for the conventional loan, since the hybrid doesn't require mortgage insurance.

30-year fixed-rate conventional with private mortgage insurance	$1,871
3/27 subprime hybrid without private mortgage insurance	$1,748

Now the payment on the subprime offering is actually lower—much lower, in fact—than the payment on a conventional loan with the mortgage insurance premium of $208 added into the monthly payment.

This approach can work for the borrower if property appreciation is expected within the first three years of the loan, at which point a borrower who has had damaged credit can have repaired it or a borrower with good credit can refinance to get the mortgage insurance premium off of the loan.

I've compared these scenarios for years, and a zero-down offering from a subprime lender can often actually be a better choice than a zero-down loan from a conventional source! There are a couple of considerations when making such a choice, however, and one of them is the likelihood of refinancing a zero-down note sometime in the future.

With the zero-down conventional loan in this example, the $208 mortgage insurance premium is a little hard to swallow. The borrower will want to refinance out of that mortgage insurance at some point down the road, usually sooner rather than later.

The very same thing can be said for the 3/27 hybrid ARM. Before the initial three-year rate expires, the borrower wants to refinance out of that product and into a conventional one. A typical adjustment after the first three years on a hybrid ARM can be 6.00 percent or more on top of the one-year Treasury index that the loan is based upon. That means that cute little 7.50 percent interest rate could zoom as high as 11 or 12 percent at the beginning of year 4. That's plenty of motivation to get out of that loan before the three years have expired.

In the meantime, hopefully, the property has appreciated enough to get rid of mortgage insurance in both cases. At least, that's the plan. So if refinancing two or three years hence is pretty much a given, why not take the subprime loan? That's a good question, one that my borrowers have answered by opting for the hybrid ARM more often than not. The ones that decided to stay with conventional financing simply didn't want any surprises at the end.

This example doesn't work with seriously damaged credit, however. Those with credit scores all the way down to 580 will be looking at rates for the same zero-down 3/27 loans approaching 9.00 percent or higher. But there are plenty of offerings in the subprime market for those without any down payment money. It's just that few people know about them.

Why do people with bad credit take out zero-down loans? Why

wouldn't they? If a house comes up on the market and someone has damaged credit, who can blame that person for wanting to buy the house regardless? If your debt ratios are in line with the loan product and you feel comfortable with those ratios, then by all means go ahead and buy the property.

Credit problems are typically temporary, and one of the best ways to get a credit report back on track is to begin paying on a new mortgage. Subprime zero-down loans can be one of the best ways to start for people who have found themselves in bad credit situations.

CHAPTER 11

Borrowing from a 401(k), an IRA, or Other Assets

Borrowing from a 401(k) has been around for a long, long time—about as long as 401(k) retirement plans themselves. And this is a great way to buy a house if you're lucky enough to have a 401(k) at your job. Using an IRA to buy a home is a more recent introduction to help foster homeownership.

A 401(k) program allows a person to have a certain percentage of her gross income deducted from her paycheck and put directly into a retirement account. These funds are deposited tax-free, and the employer may or may not contribute to the account. This is a great way to save for retirement, but it can also be a great way to help buy a house.

When you borrow from a 401(k) to buy a house, it's more like transferring assets in lieu of putting no money down on a home. Yes, you had to put some money down, but you had the funds elsewhere and simply transferred those funds as a down payment. The difference between buying a home using money from a savings account and buying it using money from a 401(k) is that the funds in the 401(k) get "paid back" automatically through paycheck withholdings each month. With a savings account, you will have to begin saving all over again to replace those funds with after-tax income.

A 401(k) has a "vested" balance, the amount that is fully owned by the borrower. Vesting can take place when an employee has worked a minimum period of time at his job or has contributed a certain amount of funds. If there is a 401(k) balance of $50,000 and the employee is only 50 percent vested, then she has access to only $25,000. If the employee is 100 percent vested, she has rights to all of the funds.

To buy a house using a 401(k), you have to contact your 401(k) plan administrator and ask if the 401(k) plan allows for withdrawals. Most do, but on certain terms. Most allow you to withdraw up to 50 percent of your vested balance and will make you pay back the fund each month under predetermined loan parameters. A common 401(k) loan looks like this:

Vested balance	$50,000
Loan available	$25,000
Terms	Prime plus 2% for 48 months

If you borrowed $25,000 on those terms, and if prime today were 6.00 percent, then your monthly payment would be $610.

But wait—if those funds are yours in the first place, how can you "borrow" from yourself? That's a good question, but that's precisely how these loans are set up. The amount of money you want to borrow is transferred as equity for a down payment. That down payment is replaced each month by your monthly payment of $610 per month. Think of it as an 80/20, but you have only one mortgage on the home.

The reason you can borrow only 50 percent of your vested balance is for the protection of the fund. If you default on your 401(k) loan or you leave your current employer and its plan, the 50 percent that you still have is there to cover any loan balance you've yet to pay off.

The benefits of borrowing against a 401(k) are many, but if you're unsure of how this would affect your retirement plans or just have questions in general, you need to speak with a financial planner and fully understand the impact of taking money out of a 401(k) fund to buy a home.

The first drawback is that the minute you take money out of your 401(k), you're no longer earning a return on that money. If the markets are doing well and your money is tied up in a home, that's bad. If you borrowed $25,000 and you could have earned 10 percent per year on that amount, then you have simply lost that investment opportunity.

On the other hand, if you took out $25,000 and the markets in general turned sour, then you could have protected those funds against losses by using them as collateral for a loan.

A benefit of 401(k) loans is that applicants are rarely turned down. If a borrower is fully vested and employed full time, and if the program allows employees to borrow to buy a home, then the typical 401(k) loan is approved. No credit report is pulled or debt ratios calculated—you just get the money. Tax- and penalty-free.

If you have a 401(k) program with an employer that you no longer work for, it's possible that you may have full access to the fund. For example, suppose you leave ABC Company and have a $30,000 401(k) balance. You can usually elect to keep the money at the company and let its 401(k) plan administrator continue to manage the account for you. Nothing much changes, other than the fact that you'll no longer contribute to the plan as you did in the past and your employer won't, of course, continue to deposit funds into the account.

If your 401(k) is a rollover and is deposited into another account that you control, then you can get at those funds almost anytime you want to, as long as you pay income tax and a 10 percent early withdrawal penalty if you're under 59$\frac{1}{2}$ years young. That's rough. Don't use those funds unless it's absolutely necessary, and even then only at the suggestion of your financial planner, CPA, or some other person who is well versed in personal finance.

There is, however, something that the IRS calls "hardship" withdrawals, meaning that under certain circumstances, a person can withdraw funds without penalty. Circumstances permitting hardship withdrawals typically include paying for unreimbursed medical expenses, paying college tuition or education costs, or preventing a foreclosure on your home or eviction from your residence.

But for this to be permitted, you'll need to show that you're pretty much "tapped out" across the board and have no other resources. While you can certainly use a withdrawal to buy a home, it's not your best choice.

You can borrow from your 401(k) without penalty and without paying income taxes, then repay that money to your retirement plan. Each month, as you pay back your loan, you're also replenishing your retirement account. You got your house, and you didn't put any money down—you simply transferred some equity, and you're paying it back in manageable monthly installments.

A common question about 401(k) loans is, "Okay, I get it, but does my monthly payment now go toward figuring my debt ratio, and will the higher ratio stop me from getting a house?"

No. Okay, yes, your debt ratios are increased, but lenders realize that you're paying yourself back—much like a bank savings plan—not paying some other third party. If your ratios push you a few points over a guideline, don't sweat it. If your ratios jump from 35 percent to 50 percent, you need to talk to your loan officer to get a better idea of how you're going to get where you need to go.

Recent changes to individual retirement accounts, or IRAs, allow for restricted use of those funds to buy a home. When you use an IRA, it's not a loan; you're transferring funds with no fixed repayment method.

A borrower can be hit hard with taxes and penalties for an early withdrawal from an IRA. But the government has allowed people to cash in all or part of an IRA to help buy a home under special circumstances.

The IRA funds can be used by first-time home buyers only, defined as someone who hasn't owned a home in the previous two full years before the closing date on the new home. The home must also be used as a primary residence; the funds can't be used to buy vacation homes or rental properties.

The IRA funds can be used by you, your spouse, your kids, your grandkids, or a direct relative of you or your spouse, such as a parent or grandparent. As long as someone in those categories is a first-time home buyer using the described definition, then it's okay to use IRA funds, penalty-free, to help buy a home.

One big difference between using an IRA and using a 401(k) is that the IRA allows only a $10,000 maximum withdrawal ($20,000 if a husband and wife buy together). While that may not sound like a lot, it's typically enough for a down payment and closing costs. Another big difference is that there is rarely a requirement that a 401(k) loan be limited to first-time home buyers; it's available to anyone who qualifies under the withdrawal guidelines.

A pledged asset mortgage, or PAM, is a way to use equity in other liquid assets, such as stocks, bonds, or mutual funds, as security for buying a home instead of providing a down payment. There are advantages and disadvantages to this type of mortgage, but because one needs to have an investment or retirement portfolio to begin with, it's not the most common form of financing.

The advantage is that instead of cashing in stocks or mutual funds, the borrower pledges those securities as collateral in order to buy the new home.

There is no requirement that the funds be used only by first-time home buyers. In fact, PAMs are rarely used by the novice homeowner; it is usually only those with significant portfolios who can afford such a method.

The typical PAM asks for a stock account equal to 30 to 40 percent of the purchase price to be either opened or pledged. If you already have a stock account, the lender (who is also your stockbroker or mutual fund adviser) asks that you set aside a certain amount of stocks and pledge those securities for the new home.

If a home sells for $400,000 and the PAM requires a 30 percent pledge, then you'll need to open up a stock fund for 30 percent of that amount, or $120,000. The assets pledged can be anything that's publicly traded, and also mutual fund accounts, CDs, or bonds. If the buyer does not have a current stock account with the lender, instead of putting 20 or 30 percent down to buy the home, she instead transfers assets into the stockbroker's account, and the stockbroker then issues a mortgage.

It's important to note a few things about a PAM. First, your new mortgage will be for 100 percent of the sales price. And that's with one great big loan, not a piggyback or other financing. You will be getting a zero-down loan while doing nothing more than moving some of your assets around. A neat benefit is that a PAM is one of the few zero-down loan programs that don't require mortgage insurance.

Another feature of PAMs is that you can usually continue to actively trade the pledged portfolio just like any other fund. Just because you pledged a certain amount of funds as collateral to buy the house doesn't mean that the money goes into some sort of "blind" trust where you no longer have control over those funds. You do, at least at either your or your stockbroker's discretion.

If you have stocks or other qualifying funds, you may want to consider a PAM, especially if you had intended to cash in those stocks and use the funds for a down payment and closing costs. If you cash in stocks, you could have a capital gain on which you'll have to pay taxes, but if you transfer those stocks as pledged collateral, you're not cashing anything in, so the capital gains tax may not apply.

A drawback is that you may have to adjust your pledge as time goes on. Let's say that you pledged 1,000 shares of Dell stock at $30 each, or $30,000. You then buy a $100,000 home with that pledge and finance 100 percent of the sales price. Later on down the road, the Dell stock takes a hit and drops to $25 per share. You've just "lost" $5,000. If your pledge requires a 30 percent collateral amount, then you can expect a telephone call from your broker or whoever is controlling your PAM account wanting more money.

It's like a margin call on a stock: Once the value dips below a certain amount and stays there, your lender will ask that the pledge amount be returned to the appropriate level. That can be a negative with a PAM, but if the arrangement is properly managed, such calls are rare.

PAMs aren't that widely known, but they are available at most investment institutions, and even Fannie Mae has a PAM program. If you're interested in a PAM and think you can qualify, first contact your investment adviser or lender for details. If the response you get from your loan officer is something like, "What's a PAM?" then you'll need to find a loan officer who knows how to work these programs. Most loan officers who are familiar with PAMs have relationships with professional investors or certified financial planners and refer business to each other.

If you have the assets to take advantage of a PAM, then this might be one of the easiest, most cost-effective ways to buy a property, be it a primary residence or for a rental. This is truly a zero-down program that's as competitive in the marketplace as any program.

Seller Carry, Lease-Purchase, Wraps, and Land Contracts

Seller Carry Notes

These types of purchase are usually reserved for those who are having difficulty finding conventional financing and do not want to pay the higher rates associated with subprime lending or with "stated income" mortgage loans.

They also require a motivated seller who is both willing and able to provide the financing. If the local real estate market is moving along at a brisk pace, then finding a seller who is willing to settle for monthly payments instead of one big, fat check at closing may be difficult.

Rarely will you find such a situation in an area with average to strong home sales. What's the incentive for a seller to go through the hassles of carrying a mortgage for someone who didn't want to make a down payment? Seller-carry notes, also called seller carrybacks, are most often found in areas where real estate is moving slowly or when the seller needs to move right away and doesn't have a whole lot of time to negotiate too many things.

A seller could be motivated to do this if the real estate market is slow. In an effort to move the property, the seller could offer "owner financing" as an incentive to buy. Of course, such an ad is generally answered by buyers who are having financing issues, for whatever reason.

A seller also will need to own the property free and clear, with no other liens or interests filed against the home. If a homeowner sells a home with a mortgage on it, the mortgage holder wants its money upon sale. If you don't have any money for a down payment and aren't getting other financing, there's no money available to pay off the mortgage holder.

Seller-carry notes are financed solely by the seller. The terms and conditions of your new loan from the seller can pretty much be anything you agree to, but typically they will be similar to a regular mortgage with regard to the amount borrowed, the rate, the payment, and so on.

Okay, I know that simply having the seller finance the note sounds like an easy way to get into a house with zero down. Finding people who are willing to do this can be quite a challenge, however, and it can take some legwork on your part.

You may see a property advertised as "owner carry," or your Realtor can search for homes in the market that have "seller financing" or "owner carry" as items for negotiation. But if you do find a home where the seller is considering financing the buyer, then you can expect a few things to happen.

First, the seller will want to see a credit report and a history of paying on time. The credit report is fairly simple, but you also need to make sure you're paying your landlord on time if you're renting or making your mortgage payments on time every month. Remember that you're asking the seller to sell you the house with nothing down and to carry the financing to boot. You need to package yourself just as you would for a job interview.

One of the most powerful ways to sweeten a zero-down, seller-carry offer is to provide copies of cancelled checks to your old landlord for the past two years. All too often, people who have yet to buy their first home pay their rent in cash or with money orders and never keep the receipts. If this is your situation, begin paying your rent with either cashier's checks or bank checks if at all possible.

When a lender verifies rent payments, it does so by using third-party verification. Handwritten receipts or a letter from a landlord rarely works.

However, copies of cancelled checks, meaning both sides, will show timely rent payments.

Have you been at your current employer for quite some time? Then don't forget to put that on your "résumé" as well. When someone has been at a job for several years, this can show stability in earnings and a level of responsibility not seen with "job hoppers" who change jobs every six months or so.

You might also want to sweeten your offer with either a higher price or a better rate of return. If the seller is willing to carry a note on the home, then he will want to get a good rate of return. If the seller is asking $150,000, then offer $155,000. Or if, for example, the current rate of return on a local certificate of deposit is 4.00 percent, then offer an 8.00 percent return. Whatever it is that you offer, make it worth the seller's while.

A neat benefit of a seller carry with zero down is that there is no mortgage insurance involved—you're working with a private party. Using a 7.50 percent interest rate with zero down and a $150,000 loan, the monthly payment for a 30-year fixed-rate mortgage is $1,048. Now add the mortgage insurance premium of $125 and your total monthly payment goes to $1,173.

If, instead, you offer the seller an above-market rate of 8.50 percent on a $150,000 loan, your monthly payment is $1,153—lower than that on a conventional zero-down loan. But to get such a sweet deal, you'll need some patience and preparation. If your credit needs to be repaired before you explore seller-carry notes, then get it repaired. If there are any questionable credit or employment issues in your past, get them addressed and fixed before you go too much further.

Many seller-carry loans will have a "balloon" feature, whereby after a certain period of time, the entire loan balance becomes due and the owner will have to refinance the owner's note or otherwise pay it off.

This is very common for buyers who just barely miss out on conventional financing for some reason. It gives the buyers time to repair their credit, get a higher-paying job, have the property increase in value, or any combination thereof.

Since this is a private transaction, you'll want to make sure that the sale takes place properly, that everything is legal and ownership is transferred according to the laws of your state. For that, you'll need an attorney to review any legal documents and also to make sure that there's a title insurance policy in there somewhere. Every lender wants a clean title report upon making a brand new mortgage, and you do the same. Who pays for this is up for negotiations, but all too often in private transactions, title insurance is forgotten about, and the buyer finds out later on that there is another outstanding lien on the property that she wasn't aware of.

Make this a requirement of sale if at all possible. If you, in turn, ever sell the property to someone else and the transfer to you wasn't handled correctly or previous liens and interests weren't addressed, then you could find yourself with a mess on your hands.

Seller-carry, zero-down products can be one of the best things on the market—they're just much harder to find.

Lease-Purchase

A lease-purchase, sometimes called a "lease with an option to buy" or "lease option," is a promise to buy a property at a specified price, typically at a specified date a couple of years in the future. Often a portion of the rent is held back each month and saved up by the seller to go toward your down payment. This is a great way to get into a home you really want if you don't have down payment money saved and you can find a willing seller. But there are some things you need to watch out for.

The most important may be your monthly payment. Let's say that you agree to buy the house you're moving into for $150,000, and your rent is $1,000 per month. The seller has agreed to withhold $300 each month to go toward your purchase price as a down payment. Your lease-purchase agreement states that you will provide financing at the end of 24 months, meaning that you're going to pay off the seller by getting a new mortgage.

After two years, the seller has saved up $7,200 for you. But here comes the tricky part: the seller can save only the amount above the current market rent for that property. If the house could rent for $1,000 a month and the seller is putting aside $300 each month for you, then in effect your rent is only $700, or $300 below market rentals in that area. The seller is not saving anything for you, but instead is giving you a gift each month in the amount of $300. Sellers can't give gifts to buyers for their down payments.

If the market rent for a similar house in your neighborhood is $1,000 and you want to save $300 every month, then your monthly payments need to be $1,300, not $1,000. At the end of your lease period, when your lender credits you for the monies you've saved, it's this amount that the lender will use.

How do you determine market rent? Well, maybe you can find an appraiser to make a market rent determination, but that will cost you about $300. An easier way is to simply cut out rental advertisements in the classified section of your newspaper that show how much homes in your area are renting for.

Some lenders may also require that the extra funds you pay each month be kept in a separate account by the seller and not commingled with the seller's personal funds. If this is not a requirement, then bona fide proof of how much you saved each month will be. If you do these two things, there should be little argument regarding how much money is available for your down payment.

Fannie Mae also has a lease-purchase program, as does Freddie Mac. Under these programs, nonprofit groups buy the house, then lease it back to you on terms similar to those a seller would use. The lease-purchase arrangement is little different other than that the owner of the property is typically a nonprofit organization or state agency devoted to getting people into homes that they otherwise may not have qualified for.

There are certain maximum income requirements and other guidelines, but these loans are an option if you can find them. To locate a nonprofit agency that participates in these programs, either contact the agencies listed in Appendix C at the back of this book or visit www.fannie mae.com or www.freddiemac.com for a list of participating organizations.

Wrap Mortgages

A "wrap" mortgage or "wrap-around" is so called because it "wraps" around another mortgage. For example, suppose a seller wishes to sell a home and has found a buyer who can't quite qualify. The seller of the property arranges to sell the house and act as the lender, similar to seller financing.

But with a wrap mortgage, the original note doesn't go away. Instead, the seller takes the monthly payment from the buyers and uses those funds to pay the original mortgage. There are essentially two mortgages on one house.

How can that happen? Actually, it can't. Or shouldn't. Almost every loan in existence today does not allow a wrap mortgage. There are specific instructions when new loans are issued that if title, or ownership of the property, changes hands, then the note currently on the property becomes due in full.

That means if you buy a house with a wrap, then the terms of the original note have been violated and the mortgage must be paid off immediately. The trick with wraps, of course, is not notifying the original lender of the sale. And that trick can get you in trouble.

Let's say that you bought a house with a wrap and dutifully paid your mortgage on time. Let's also say that your seller, who is supposed to send your mortgage payment to the original lender, doesn't do so. Guess what? You lose. The original seller still owns the property, regardless of any arrangement you may have made privately. If the original mortgage becomes delinquent, then the home can be foreclosed upon. Even though you had a sales contract and made your payments on time, the home wasn't yours. It was transferred illegally, and you lost not only your monthly payments, but any equity you may have thought you accrued.

Land Contracts

Land contracts are "rent-to-own" arrangements that work similarly to other installment loans, such as an automobile loan. You don't own a car until the loan is paid off. After you've made all the payments, the car's title changes from your lender to you.

With a land contract, you "bought" the property, but you don't own it until the loan is all paid off, unlike the standard situation, where you own the property upon purchase, but there is another interest (your mortgage) legally filed as a claim.

Rent-to-own programs can be an option for those who have trouble qualifying for conventional or government loans, but I'll admit they're very hard to find. You really need a motivated seller to do anything with regard to a rent-to-own arrangement.

CHAPTER 13

What's in a Credit Report?

A credit report contains everything that participating financial institutions or lending companies have reported about your payment history with them. It will be broken down into three areas: who you are, how you've paid, and public records.

Who you are is any identifying information about you, including not just the name you generally use but any other forms of your name that you might have used when applying for credit. If you use the name Billy Bob Smith, Jr., it's likely that your legal name is in fact William Robert Smith, II. Or Jr. Or Willy Robert. Or Willy Bob. Or Willy Bob, Jr.

Name variations are taken from the various ways you originally applied for credit accounts. If you applied at Sears under the name of William Smith and later at Target as Bill Smith, Jr., then both name varieties will appear on your credit report. These variations are known as "aka's" or "also known as."

Your social security number is stored, along with your date of birth and where you've lived.

The second batch of information stored about you is the history of how you've paid your accounts and to whom you've paid them. The report will list, typically beginning with the most recent, the names of the businesses that have extended you credit. You will also see other information, such as what type of credit was issued: a mortgage, an automobile or other installment loan, a lease, or a revolving line of credit like that offered by a standard credit card. The credit limit on each loan will also be listed, showing the maximum amount of credit the issuer was willing to grant, along with your current balance and the highest balance you've ever had. Next to that is the good part, showing how many times you've been late, if ever.

Late payments on a credit report are listed in increments of 30 days and are commonly shown as "30 +," "60 +," "90 +," and "120 +." If a single payment was more than 30 days past the due date on your statement but less than 60 days past due, then the number 1 will appear below "30 +," showing that you've been more than 30 days late on that account one time. If there's a 3 below the "90 +," it shows that you've been more than 90 days late three times on that particular account.

This section also shows when the last payment was made and when the last late payment was made. This is the core of how your credit score is calculated, discussed in Chapter 15.

The final section includes any public records that may legally be included in your credit report. Legal entries include those that are financial in nature, such as a filing of bankruptcy or a wage-earner plan. Are there any foreclosures or financial judgments on your record? If so, they will appear in this third section.

A complete list of where you've lived will also be listed in your credit report.

Finally, and less significantly these days, there will be a list of others who have inquired into your credit along with the corresponding dates of inquiry.

Each time you apply for credit, whatever you put on your credit application is what is stored at the various credit bureaus. If you suddenly start going by "Gene" instead of "Eugene," then "Gene" will soon begin showing up on your report along with your suddenly expired "Eugene" moniker. Even people who have accidentally misspelled or had their names misspelled on a loan application will ultimately find that mistake on their reports.

If a credit card offer arrives with an extra "n" in your name—"Donna" instead of the correct spelling "Dona"—you may receive credit card offers or other solicitations with that exact same misspelling: "Welcome, Donna! You're approved!"

There are several things that are against the law to put in your credit report, and still others that you may think would be included but aren't. Credit reports can store only information identifying who you are and how you pay your bills.

Unless you apply for credit with your spouse, there won't be anything in there about whether you're married or not. There's also nothing in there regarding your medical history. You won't find your age listed on a credit report, although you may find your birth date. Part of the data identifying individuals is their birth date, and your age may be calculated from that information.

Credit information that is more than seven years old will not be on your credit report. That includes collection accounts. It's important to know that there must not have been any "activity" on the listed negative item for seven years. If an old collection account gets transferred from one agency to another, that counts as activity and can extend the permitted period by another seven years. Or you may finally pay off a collection account that showed up on your report for several years. That "paid collection" entry could be there for seven years as well.

CHAPTER 14

No Credit Versus Bad Credit

You've seen the advertisements in the newspaper or on television proclaiming, "No Credit Okay! Bad Credit Okay!" And there is indeed a difference between having no credit and having bad credit. They are not the same thing and are not interchangeable.

No credit means that you have bought nothing on credit, and so you have never established a repayment history. You have never taken out an automobile loan or a credit card. This means that if someone runs your credit report, he won't find your name or social security number, and if he did find them, the report wouldn't list any creditors.

This doesn't necessarily mean that you have in fact never had an obligation that you paid back in regular installments; it's just that these transactions were never reported to a credit bureau. If no repayment history is reported to a credit bureau, then a credit history won't be established. No credit is a whole new challenge when buying a home.

Most mortgage programs require a credit history. From a credit history, a credit score is calculated. Based on that credit score, an approval can be issued. Unfortunately, most people think that no credit history also means no home loan. But that's not true. There are alternative-credit sources.

Alternative-credit sources show that the borrower has agreed to pay someone or some business a certain amount each month for a product or a service. What sort of services? You'd be surprised. Alternative credit can be established through utility bills. How can that be?

Isn't it reasonable to assume that if someone has had telephone, water, and utility bills for the previous couple of years and has made those payments on time, that shows her ability to repay a debt? Of course it is, and there are loan programs that allow for such payment histories. FHA loans are the biggest single source for alternative-credit borrowers.

If you don't have credit established, then begin documenting your cable television, your cell phone, your electricity, your water bill—anything that you're obligated to pay each month on a certain due date.

You want to show that you have received bills for services on a regular basis and that you have paid these bills on time. How do you show that you paid these bills? Your telephone bill isn't on a credit report, but each month's bill shows when your previous month's bill was due and when you paid it. Your electricity bill reports the same thing. So does the bill for any other service or utility you subscribe to.

This is important for alternative-credit loans. While certain loan programs will accept alternative credit, it's important that the information you provide is what the lender wants to see.

For instance, if you show that, yes, you paid your electricity bill, but it was always more than 30 days past the due date, then that will be a problem. If your telephone company or cable television company shows that your services have been disconnected for any reason, then you'll have trouble qualifying.

If you're in a situation where you have no traditional credit established, remember that there are other ways to establish credit. Document your payment history and present it to your lender.

Some recent moves in the field of making loans for those with "no" credit come from credit-scoring companies. Fair Isaac Corporation, or FICO, has developed a credit-scoring system that will calculate a score using alternative credit. We'll discuss credit scores in depth in Chapter 15, but this is the first time a credit score can be assigned to someone who hasn't obtained credit from a mortgage company or finance operation.

You will be asked to provide your lender with your alternative-credit documentation covering the previous two years, and a score will then be assigned. For loans that require credit scores, this method of scoring alternative credit will work for people who haven't established credit in the traditional sense. No credit? No problem!

How to Establish Credit

If you don't have any credit and you want to establish it, you'll need to go a step further than using alternative-credit sources such as telephone and cable television bills. To establish credit, you need to buy something on credit, then make your payments on time, every time. That's it.

But how can a person establish credit if no one will grant credit without a prior credit account? It's true that there are certain credit accounts that require a traditional credit history, but there are a couple of places to get started with a credit account.

The first place to begin is most likely at a department store. Many department stores offer credit accounts and are willing to issue credit to first-timers. Don't expect a credit line in the stratosphere, though. Your first credit account is likely to have a credit limit of $250 to $500. Another option is to apply for a credit account from a gasoline company. They too may issue credit on a limited basis to those without a history.

But if you're having trouble or would rather not wonder whether or not you're going to get a credit card, then go to your bank and open up a *secured* credit card account.

A secured credit card is just like any other credit card in that it has a credit limit and when you charge something on it, you have to make monthly payments to pay it off. However, instead of having an open credit line with no collateral, you "secure" the card with cash up front.

For a secured credit card, you will need to make a cash deposit of anywhere from $250 to $5,000, whatever you choose or the bank requires, into a collateral account. This cash deposit acts as a "backup" for the bank in case of default on your part.

If your deposit is $1,000, then your credit line will be $1,000. You will then be issued your first credit card, and it will look just like any other card. When you buy something on the card, you will get a statement in the mail each month showing the required minimum monthly payment.

The minimum monthly payment is your contractual obligation to pay the bank back. If you charged $100, then your minimum monthly payment could be, say, $18.00. Your minimum monthly payment is a function of the interest rate attached to your card account.

You can pay the minimum, which includes the interest or finance charge, or you can pay a little more than that or you can pay the balance in full. It's up to you, but you need to pay at least the minimum required on or before the due date.

Most card accounts give you 25 to 30 days to make a payment by the due date, although some cards ask for the money a lot sooner. Pay very close to that due date and don't be late; if you are, you will be establishing bad credit.

In Chapter 13, we talked about how late payments show up on your credit report, showing how many payments were more than 30 days past due, 60 days past due, and so on. Those notations are for credit-reporting purposes, and lenders use them as an accepted guideline when determining "good" or "not so good" credit.

Be warned, however: Even if a payment to a credit account is less than 30 days past the due date, if it is as little as one day past the due date, the credit issuer will most likely penalize you by increasing your interest rate to much a higher level. Pay the account before the due date and you won't have those problems.

Most secured cards will return your cash deposit to you after 12 months of on-time payments and keep your credit line the same as the original amount. Continuous on-time payments and responsible credit usage will soon be rewarded with an increased credit limit (if that's what you want, of course).

After you've opened up your first credit account, you may apply for another credit account after three to six months of use. Be careful though; just because credit is available to you doesn't mean that using it is a good thing. Many a folk have gotten themselves into credit hot water, or worse, by opening up and using too many credit lines.

When you've established a track record with a credit account, you need to make certain that the lending institution is reporting your payment history to the credit bureaus. To find this out, simply ask about it while you're applying for the credit account. If the institution doesn't report, you may want to try another bank. Odds are that almost every bank will report your information, however. After all, they're members of the credit bureaus, too.

CHAPTER 15

Credit Scores

Credit scoring for mortgages is perhaps one of the single most important changes in mortgage lending over the past decade. Credit scoring is a method of assigning a number to your credit report, rating the possibility of your defaulting on a loan. The lower the score, the more likely a default, and the higher the score, the less likelihood of late payments on a loan and ultimately the less likelihood of default.

Credit scores can range from 300 to 850. Is there an average credit score? Maybe, but credit scores are fluid and can change. An "average" consumer credit score is somewhere around 720. But that doesn't mean that a score of 719 is terrible credit. Hardly. That's why you need a complete understanding of what credit scores are and what they are not.

I believe the lowest score I've ever seen was in the low 500s, and the highest I've ever seen was around 810. And I've seen a lot of loans. Frankly, I don't know if anyone can attain a "perfect" credit score, although I'm sure there are people out there who are trying—sort of like an athlete trying to get a perfect "10" in an Olympic event.

Where did credit scores come from? A company called Fair Isaac Corporation, or FICO for short, developed a numbering system that assigns a three-digit number to a credit report. All three credit bureaus use FICO, which supplies the bureaus with its credit-scoring engine.

Several factors are evaluated when calculating a score. So many points are given for no late payments, more points for how long credit has been established, more points for low balances, and so on. Points can be deducted for such things as being more than 30, 60, 90, or 120 days late on a payment, going over a credit line, or other such unfortunate events.

Scores are not based on a single event, but rather look at the previous two-year period; they evaluate a person's recent history, then assign a number to that history. That's why one negative item on a credit report may not, by itself, damage a score. However, that one negative item combined with other negative items can kill a score. I've seen excellent credit scores with an open collection account, for example. The collection account was absolutely the only negative item on the report; the person had perfect credit otherwise.

Conventional mortgages and government mortgages are not approved or denied based upon a score. There may be certain "boutique" loans such as 100 percent programs or certain first-time home buyer loans that have score requirements, but there is no such thing as a minimum credit score for a conventional or government loan.

Because credit scoring is relatively new, there are also common misunderstandings about what scores can and can't do.

When lenders pull a score for a credit determination, they receive three scores, one from each bureau. Some people falsely believe that these scores are added together, then averaged. Not true. In fact, lenders will throw out the highest score and the lowest score and use the middle one.

There is a reason for doing this. The three credit bureaus are located in three distinct regions of the United States. If an individual has lived all of his life in Oregon, for instance, all of his credit data will involve businesses and transactions in that section of the country. In this instance, TransUnion would carry most of his credit information, while Equifax in Atlanta wouldn't have as many entries. That's why even though all three bureaus use the same FICO engine, they'll almost always come up with different scores.

I've seen credit reports where one score was 760, the lowest score was 620 and the middle score was 680. A lender would use 680. Lenders feel that by using the middle number rather than the highest or the lowest, they can get a better picture of a borrower's credit profile.

If you're using another person as a co-borrower for a mortgage, such as a spouse, a friend or relative, or a business partner, then what number do lenders use? Each person on the application also has three numbers. If one person's middle score is 770 and the other person's is 570, what happens then?

Lenders won't average the scores. They have to consider the lower score just as much as they would a higher one. But the irony here is that a high score won't compensate for a low score; instead, a low score can kill a deal.

In the case of multiple borrowers on one application, lenders will use the score of the borrower who makes the most money. If the person with 770 made $5,000 per month and the person with the 570 number made $10,000 per month, guess what? The score for loan purposes is 570, not 770. Conversely, if the person with 770 made $10,000 and the one with 570 made $5,000, the lenders will use the 770 score.

But what if the incomes aren't that different or are almost the same? That's when the bad score can really hurt. There's no way around it for loans that have minimum scores.

Because the scoring engines don't isolate a single event in arriving at a particular number, paying off any negative credit items won't immediately affect a score. For example, suppose your score comes in at 620, but you need 630. When you review your credit report, you discover a recent collection account that hasn't been paid. You rush to the collection agency, pay the debt, then document the transaction and wait for your new score to be calculated. Guess what? There's little or no change. In fact, the score could actually drop a little because there was new activity on the collection item; whether it was good activity or bad activity doesn't matter.

There is considerable confusion regarding credit scores and rates. There is no one-to-one correlation between your score and the rate for conventional or government products. If you're approved for a conventional Fannie Mae loan and your score is 600, you shouldn't be paying a much higher rate than another borrower under the very same loan program with a 700 score.

In fact, many web sites make this mistake and actually post what rate you're likely to get if your credit score is such-and-such. A chart on a popular web site makes such a claim.

This chart shows that if your score is 620 to 639, your rate could be 7.00 percent, whereas with a score of 640 to 659, your rate could be 6.45 percent. That's a drop of more than half a percent. On a $200,000 mortgage, that difference in rate is $73 per month, or nearly $8,000 over the next 10 years. Still further, the table shows a rate of 5.41 percent if you're lucky enough to have a score over 760. That means a payment of $1,124, or $206 lower than that with the 7.00 percent rate.

But having closed thousands of mortgage loans, I can tell you that that's not how it works, and I think too many people simply don't apply for the best loan if they believe that their score will cost them $200 more each month. They simply wait, or they apply for a subprime loan instead.

Such information, while in general attempting to explain the importance of credit scores, make two false assumptions:

1. A change in credit score of a single point can change a rate by $^1/_2$ percent or more.
2. Credit scores are the only determining factor when handing out interest rates.

With regard to the first assumption, there are loan programs offered under guidelines different from those used by conventional or government programs. Sometimes these loans are made by private lenders who do not wish to sell the loans but instead keep them, or they involve subprime loan programs, and in these situations the credit score is in fact the determining factor in rate.

While that's true in these particular cases, however, that method of associating a rate with a particular score applies to only a small part of the available loan choices. Fannie Mae, Freddie Mac, VA, and FHA guidelines cover nearly 80 percent of the mortgages available in the marketplace today, and such rigid scoring considerations simply don't apply.

Claiming that if your score is 639 instead of 640, your payment automatically goes up by $70 on a $200,000, 30-year mortgage is nonsense.

With regard to the second assumption, while there are specific loan programs that may require a particular score, the score alone is rarely the single determining factor. I recall a client a couple of years ago who applied for a refinancing. His ratios were a little high (around 45 percent for the housing ratio); he didn't have much money in the bank, so his liquid asset count was marginal; and his credit score was low: 580.

If the online charts were correct, this person would not even get a rate quote because his score was so low. If he had paid attention to score claims, it's likely that he would have never even applied for the refinancing and lowered his monthly payments. But he got approved anyway, at rates typically reserved for those with scores of 760 or above. He got exactly the same interest rate, with exactly the same points and fees, as another client who had a score of 785, because credit scores aren't the single determining factor when getting approved for conventional or government financing; they're simply a part of the equation.

This man's loan was for $185,000, while his property was worth about $650,000, or a 28 percent loan-to-value ratio (LTV). His considerable equity was taken into consideration by the AUS, and he got the best rate available. On the other hand, if this borrower had had an appraised value of only $200,000, or an LTV of 92.5 percent, it's doubtful that he would have gotten the loan. His credit score was extremely low, but other factors played into his approval, and he got the loan he wanted.

How to Improve Your Credit Scores

If many lenders don't rely on a score for approving or denying a mortgage applicant, then why try to improve your credit score? Because a credit score isn't just a number, it's an indication of your credit standing. It's like getting an A on a test. Yes, the A is important, but it's a result of your knowing all the answers. A credit score is a result of your credit patterns. If you improve your credit score, you're really improving your credit profile.

To improve your score, you need to know what goes into making a good score and what goes into making a bad score. There is no magic formula. Well, maybe there is, but you can bet that FICO won't tell you its algorithms. However, there are some proven principles that you need to be aware of.

Pay Your Bills on Time

The first is the most obvious: paying your accounts on time. Every time. Payment history makes up 35 percent of your credit score. If you've got late payments on your credit report, make sure they're not in error, then put as much time as you can between the late payments and when you apply for a mortgage. If a score looks primarily at your most recent past, say the previous 24 months, you'll need to keep your credit report clean for at least that period.

A 30 + -day late payment hurts your score, but not as much as a 60 + -, 90 + -, or 120 + -day late payment. If your payments consistently arrive between 90 days and 120 days late, it's likely that your credit account will be closed by the credit grantor and turned over to a collection agency.

Having collection accounts hurts your score more than a 30 + -day late payment. So do charge-offs. Charge-offs occur when a lender gets tired of trying to collect from you and simply wipes the account off its books, perhaps selling it to a collection company and letting the collection company try to track you down.

Rectify Public Records

Public records can hurt your score. Do you have civil financial judgments awarded to someone else against you? Did you owe someone money and that person couldn't get it from you, so she sued you? Public records such as judgments can kill your score. So can tax liens if you haven't paid your taxes on time. Tax liens can be for property taxes or local, state, and federal income tax obligations. If you have tax bills looming or possible judgments coming down the pike, try to get them settled before they become a public record.

Avoid Bankruptcy if Possible

If you have a foreclosure, your score will dive. Is there anything worse? A bankruptcy. Still worse? A bankruptcy where the house was included in the bankruptcy. People who own homes who get into a financial mess have the choice of keeping the home out of the bankruptcy and continuing to make payments on it or including the home in the bankruptcy. Certain state laws regarding bankruptcy and primary residences can affect whether or not a home can be part of a bankruptcy. But the worst credit mark goes to a mortgage that is wiped out by a Chapter 7 or Chapter 13.

You want to begin immediately to stop making late payments, to pay off any collection accounts, and to rectify any public records. If you do not do these things, your score, along with your credit, will never improve.

Increase Your Available Credit

The next greatest impact on a credit score is what is called *available credit*. Various reports indicate that this single item makes up about 30 percent of the credit-scoring model. Do good on the available credit aspect and you've affected nearly a third of your score.

Available credit is the amount of credit available to you compared to the amount actually owed, in percent. If you have a credit line of $10,000 on a credit card and you owe $8,000, then you have 20 percent available credit.

There is a magic number for available credit. That number is 70 percent. You need to have 70 percent of your available credit lines ready, willing, and able to charge against. That means that you should strive to get your balance to 30 percent of your credit lines, leaving you with a 70 percent available credit number. If you have $20,000 in credit limits on various cards, 30 percent of $20,000 is $6,000. Likewise, if your credit lines are $100,000, then $30,000 is your target number. You should keep as many credit lines as possible open with low balances.

If you think about the 30 percent balance for a moment in terms of credit responsibility, how will a lender really, really know that you're going to pay it back if you've never charged anything? That's a good question. And in terms of calculating a credit score, that's exactly the question the scoring model wants answered. By establishing credit lines, using them, and then paying them back on time, you've hit three very important bits of score calculation. Not only were you creditworthy enough to be granted credit in the first place, but you were also responsible with that line by not charging up to the limit, and the amounts you did in fact charge, you paid back on time, every time. You verified your credit patterns by deeds and not words.

Let's look at that for a moment. If you're trying to improve your score, you need to look at your credit report, look at your available credit, then begin to methodically pay your balances down to about one-third of your limits. Concentrate on one account at a time when doing this, first choosing your highest-limit account with the highest interest rate. Pay that card or credit line down aggressively until you reach the magic percentage, then work on another account.

But whatever you do, don't pay off accounts completely, then cancel the account altogether. This will actually hurt rather than help your score. It used to be that creditors wanted applicants to close unused accounts. In fact, I recall asking borrowers to close out accounts before I could approve their loan. The logic worked this way: If a borrower had high debt ratios or her ratios were reaching acceptable limits and she had an open line of credit, it was possible that the borrower would get approved for the loan, then charge up to the maximum on all her cards, then suddenly, wham-o! Her ratios would go through the roof and she wouldn't be able to pay her mortgage any longer.

This happened all the time, especially where I was in California, where home prices were higher than in most parts of the country and people were forced to stretch their ratios more. People with absolutely sterling credit would be asked to close out one or more accounts before a loan would be approved. It sounds silly, but in fact that was good advice back then. People were asked to review their credit reports periodically for the standard stuff, such as mistakes or other people's names on their reports, but to also look for any old credit lines or department store cards they had forgotten about and to close them down.

Today, credit scores are much more important than how many lines of credit are open to you. Remember that one of the most important things you can do to improve your credit score is to keep your balances around one-third of your available credit lines. If you close out an account and still have balances, you're messing with your desired percentage.

Let's say you have three cards, each with a $10,000 credit line, and you owe a total of $5,000. Your available credit is $30,000, and your balance is $5,000. You have an 83 percent available credit number. Not bad.

Now, if you close two of those cards, your credit line is reduced to $10,000, while your balance stays at $5,000. Your available credit zooms to 50 percent. This will hurt your score. By closing accounts without making subsequent adjustments in balances, your score will be worse than before, when you had unused balances.

Another event that can affect a credit score is called *credit inquiries.* A credit inquiry is someone else looking into your credit report. Multiple credit inquiries will hurt your score if those inquiries are for different types of accounts.

Getting your own free credit report is an inquiry, but it's a consumer inquiry and doesn't affect your credit score. Going to different automobile dealerships and having each dealer look into your credit is considered a single inquiry, even though five dealerships may have pried into your score. An inquiry is a credit review for a single event. If you're buying one car, not five, during a particular period of time, that's only one inquiry.

Likewise, if you're applying for a mortgage to buy a new house and you apply to three different mortgage companies, that would be considered only one inquiry, not three, because you're looking for just one mortgage.

If you refinanced last year, then later decided to sell your home and apply for a new mortgage, that would be considered two inquiries because you were applying for two different loans at different times. That can hurt your score.

Having more inquiries on your report could indicate that you're getting yourself into financial trouble down the road. If you're opening up a credit line to buy yourself a new boat to use at your lake house, that might be just fine. But if you're opening up credit lines to pay for stuff you simply don't have the money for, you may be hurting your score.

If you're opening up new credit lines and using them for things you really don't need, or if you're using cards to pay for everyday items, then you're hurting your score. In fact, if you don't change that pattern, there's financial disaster down the road.

Probably the best way to improve your score is to continue doing the things that make up a good score. If you already have a good score, then simply do the exact same things that got you that excellent score. Many times, when people first enter the world of credit, they are surprised to find that someone will lend them money when they don't have any.

I can think of a young lady who graduated from college and got her first job. She soon applied for a department store credit card at the mall to buy some furniture for her new apartment. She liked the idea of paying $50 a month and getting $1,000 worth of furniture.

Soon, she got an offer in the mail to apply for a gasoline credit card, which she did, then soon thereafter her bank offered her a credit card as well. After a year had passed and she had made her monthly payments on time, she was thinking about buying her first condo. She pulled her credit report and saw that her credit score was 790. She was floored. She had done nothing more than open up three accounts, charge something on them, and then pay them back.

What she did next is a common mistake that people make: She went nuts. Since her score was so high, any lender or credit card company would grant her a credit line. So she applied for a couple more cards with still more available credit. She used it to go on the trip she thought she deserved, since she'd never gone to Europe before. She went to Italy and

Greece, and if I recall correctly, she also went to Paris. She was gone for nearly a month, and she charged all of it on her two new cards.

After a few months of making monthly payments that were much higher than she was used to, she began to feel pinched every time she paid the bills. In fact, her bills were so high that she found it uncomfortable to live from paycheck to paycheck, so she began to make only the minimum payments on her cards.

Not long after that, she found herself going out on the town using her credit cards instead of using her debit card or paying cash like she used to. Her available balances began to approach zero. In fact, on some of her accounts, she charged over her limit, which automatically triggered a higher interest rate on her cards.

Other lenders found out about these above-limit charges by making periodic reviews of her credit report. They too began charging her a higher rate. She struggled for quite some time, but she was never late on any of her payments.

She finally got around to finding the condo she wanted and was stunned when she looked at her credit. It was demolished. Her credit scores had dropped below 600 within a 10-month period. She also didn't have any money for a down payment, which limited the types of loans that were available to her. She was crushed. But she did the right thing— she waited until she got back on her feet. She concentrated on paying down her balances before she did any other credit shopping.

She had had such a good credit rating because she was responsible with her credit, didn't go overboard, and kept her balances low in relation to her credit lines. If she had continued to do the things that got her good credit in the first place instead of going crazy with it, she would have been in her house much sooner. The best way to keep good credit is to do the very same things that got you that good credit in the first place.

CHAPTER 16

How to Repair Credit

Okay, so the damage has been done. How does one fix a credit report once bad things have happened? There are various ways to fix your credit, but let's address ways that you can't fix it. You can't fix credit by lying about it.

You may have seen the ads, especially if you happen to be a little more sensitive to such solicitations because in fact you have damaged credit. These ads read something like "Get great credit . . . start all over and wipe out bad credit!" Be careful about such tempting ads; most likely, what they're offering is against the law.

Some companies advertise that they can erase your bad credit through legal means. Maybe. What they try to do is to issue you a new identity, by either changing your name, applying for a new social security number, or both. There's certainly nothing wrong with a name change; it happens in courts all across the country. You make an application for a name change, present your case to the court, and, if you played your cards right and the judge agrees with your request—guess what, a new you.

Sort of. You still have to have a social security number, so the company, illegally, tells you how to get a new social security number using your new name. Presto-chango, there's not only a new name but a new social security number. The old you appears to have gone away—but not really.

Let's assume that in fact you do get a new identity. Then the trick is to open up a credit account or two, just as you did when you opened up your first credit account. You apply for a secured card, or maybe a department store credit account. Then you charge something, then pay it back. After a year or two, you've established a credit report under your new name and your new social security number. Then you apply for a home loan.

Here is where it gets bad. The mortgage application, and other credit applications, by the way, asks you specifically if you've "ever been known by any other name." So what do you do? Do you say yes, then tell the lender who you used to be, and the lender finds out that you had terrible credit (that's getting worse every day because of your negligence), or do you lie and say no?

You're screwed either way. If you lie and say no, then you've just committed a felony. If you tell the truth and say yes, then your lender will research who you were and use your old credit history to decline your loan. Don't pay anyone any money who promises to wipe out your credit legally. There's no such thing when it comes to applying for a mortgage.

But guess what? There are better, easier, and legal ways to repair your credit, and you can do this by yourself as well.

There are also businesses that advertise that they can help you repair your credit without wiping out your old identity and inventing a new one. These companies will charge you a fee to tell you how to repair credit or send you a course or make you buy the CD that explains all the secrets of credit repair. You don't need those. You bought this book.

Credit repair is accomplished by:

Ordering your credit reports and looking for errors

Correcting those errors

Paying off collection accounts, judgments, or bad debts

Paying your account balances down

Paying your accounts on time

Waiting

Notice that I didn't mention anything about writing "letters of explanation" about your side of credit events, nor is there any mention of the effect of sending overnight packages to dispute such items within a 30-day period.

Credit statutes require credit bureaus to store letters written by consumers to explain or otherwise tell their side of a credit story. If a credit report shows a late payment on an automobile account, then the consumer, if he desires, can compose a statement that must be included with the file. That way, when a potential creditor reviews the credit report and sees a late payment, but also notices that the consumer has placed a letter about that payment in the file, then the potential creditor has the opportunity to read the explanation.

"Dear Credit Bureau: I am disputing the late payment on my automobile loan. I am writing this letter to state that I in fact mailed the check way before the due date and do not know why my credit report says that it's late." Do you think that's powerful? I don't, and neither would a lender. In fact, explanation letters on file do little, if anything, to help a credit report. Don't waste your time. Lenders don't read credit reports any longer; they look at credit scores, and no one takes the time to individually read anything with regard to a credit report.

Another old trick when trying to repair credit is the "30-day rule." The law requires that if a credit bureau can't prove a negative item in the credit file within 30 days, then that item must be removed from the report altogether.

There are various versions of this theme, but all of them involve disputing the negative item, reporting the dispute using an overnight courier to get a signed receipt, then waiting until 30 days are up, hoping all the while that the bureau won't find the proof needed and will have to remove the negative item. Some 30-day tricks involve having a return address outside of the United States where the mail or any other physical correspondence would take longer to reach, eating away at the so-called holy grail of 30 days.

Still other methods involve deluging the bureau with multiple requests, hoping that it will fail on at least one of them and will be required to erase the negative data. Such practices may occasionally work, and there are probably thousands of places online that will help you (and take your money all the while) through the process, but the bottom line is this: Don't expect things that are true to be taken off your credit report.

So how do you fix your credit if it's been hurt? Get your credit report. You are entitled by law to a free credit report from all three major bureaus every year. It used to be that you could get your report only if you had been turned down for credit, but that's not the case any longer. You can get a free report. And you can get your report directly from the credit bureaus.

Your reports are available from one single online source at www .annualcreditreport.com. If you don't have Web access, call 1-877-322-8228 or write:

Annual Credit Report Request Service
P.O. Box 105281
Atlanta, GA 30348-5281

Now you're ready to begin the healing process.

First, scan your report for mistakes. The first possibility is that someone else's information is on your credit report. If your name is Bob Jones, then it's possible that information on another Bob Jones is on your report. Are you a Jr., Sr., II, or IV? Again, look for accounts that don't belong to you.

Now look for any late payments that show up in the 30+, 60+, 90+, and 120+ columns. If you see any, you can see when those lates were reported right on the report. If the report states that last May you were more than 60 days late on your student loan, then find that statement along with your check or draft and compare what you have with what is being reported.

Are there other errors on the report? Are there any public records, such as bankruptcies or foreclosures, that shouldn't be there? The first step in repairing credit is to look for the things that are easiest to correct—the mistakes.

Fixing a mistake does take a little effort. You can't just call the credit

bureau and leave a message on its voicemail or shoot an e-mail to customer service. And a letter won't do any good, either. Credit bureaus
report only what's been given to them. They do not establish loan terms
or collect monthly payments. Remember, they're simply a repository
where other businesses report and share information. What you can do,
however, is provide proof that there's been a mistake and then present it
to the bureau.

Sending a dispute letter is not the same thing as proof. A dispute
letter does nothing more than perhaps make a notation in the file that
the information is being disputed. It doesn't remove the information
or otherwise correct an error. You must be able to provide third-party
verification that there's an error.

A third-party verification is something from someone or some business that backs up your story. Did you make a payment on the first, but
the lender is saying it was a month late? Then make a copy of the cancelled check, front and back, along with the statement and present it as
evidence that, yes, the payment was made on time, and you can prove it
by the cancellation date on the check.

Presenting this to the credit bureau or even to the lender or creditor
itself should usually resolve the issue. But making a complaint or calling
someone's customer service number for a "he said, she said" routine
won't cut it.

Now that you've ordered your free report and corrected any errors,
you need to address the bad stuff that really did happen. If you have past
due payments, pay them immediately. If you have collection accounts,
pay them immediately. Judgments? Ditto. Deficiencies? Pay them or negotiate them away.

Deficiencies are amounts that you still owe, even though you don't
own the collateral any longer. The most common deficiency comes from
automobile loans. When a car is repossessed because of back payments
and there is still money owed on the automobile loan, most consumers
think, "Well, at least I don't have to mess with that car payment any
longer." But that's a mistake; they still owe the money. Yes, the finance
company took the car, but sometimes the value of the car is much less
than the balance of the note.

For example, let's say a car worth $5,000 has an outstanding balance of $10,000. The owner quit making payments on the car, and the car was repossessed. The finance company sold the car at an auction for $5,000, but that leaves a balance of $5,000 still owed the finance company. This is a deficiency, and once a deficiency is on your report, it's hard to get it off.

After correcting errors and paying off back debts, it's time to pay down those balances. Don't charge any more. Keep those payments as low as possible. If you have several charge accounts, it can get confusing as to which account to pay down first. Many people simply spread the payments around all their accounts.

This in fact does little, and it can take forever to get balances down. Instead, pay the very minimum on most accounts and concentrate on the account with the largest balance and the highest rate. Pay that account down aggressively. After that account is paid down to about a third of the balance, tackle the next highest balance with the next highest interest rate and concentrate on paying that balance down by two-thirds as well.

How long does all this take? That depends. If you've a lot of repairing to do and a lot of balances to pay down, it will probably take some time. After all, it took some time to get you there in the first place, did it not? But have a little patience here. After all the mistakes are corrected, bad debts paid off, and high balances paid down, wait about 24 months for your credit to get back to "prewar" status.

CHAPTER 17

Mortgage Loans and Bankruptcies

Bankruptcy. It's probably the ugliest word in credit. It can be embarrassing, too. No one wants a bankruptcy. But in fact, bad things do happen; things can get out of a consumer's control, and he can no longer pay his debts. But life isn't over just because you've had a bankruptcy. In fact, a bankruptcy often gives someone a fresh, new start in her financial life.

I will not advocate filing for bankruptcy. That is something for you, with counsel, to decide. I am simply telling you what will happen if you do decide to file for bankruptcy and what can happen if you've already filed. Bankruptcies are not a coffin nail when it comes to getting a home loan. Unfortunately, too many people think otherwise and either don't apply for a mortgage for the rest of their lives or think that they have to wait at least seven years to get a decent home loan. Not true.

First, it's important to understand the differences between the types of bankruptcy that are available for consumers to file: bankruptcy code Chapters 7 and 13.

Chapter 7 is a complete discharge of all secured and unsecured debt. No longer do you owe any money to anyone (with a few exceptions, such as back taxes, alimony or child support, and student loans); you have a clean slate. There are some serious guidelines about bankruptcies, and they also vary by state law, so your attorney needs to tell you about the specifics that apply to you.

You may also be able to keep your home, and, of course, you have to have a car to get to work, so there are allowances to make sure that filing for bankruptcy doesn't also mean that you're homeless without a car.

Chapter 13, the other form of personal bankruptcy, is sometimes called the "wage earner" plan. When you go to bankruptcy court under a Chapter 13 filing, the court trustee will arrange for your monthly obligations to be paid to your various creditors over time, rather than wiping them out altogether. Instead of making payments to your credit card companies or other financial institutions, you make monthly payments to the trustee, who then oversees payments to the creditors.

Purely from the standpoint of qualifying for a home loan, neither form of filing is better than the other. One would think that a lender would look more kindly on a Chapter 13 filing than a Chapter 7, but in reality lenders view them much the same way.

Instead of looking at "which type," lenders look at "how long has it been since it was discharged?" A Chapter 13 filing may take two or three years to be discharged. Or longer, up to five years. After a Chapter 7 filing, two to three years may pass, during which time credit is being rebuilt. There are exceptions to this, such as subprime lenders, who look at the actual filing date of the Chapter 13 instead of the discharge date.

Certain loan programs that take bankruptcies into consideration may make it a requirement that there be one year, two years, or whatever the institution deems important since the discharge date. If you filed for Chapter 7, you could be eligible for a particular mortgage two years later, but if you filed for Chapter 13 and two years later you're still paying it off, you're still two more years away from that same home loan. I don't know if that's fair or not fair, but that's the way it is.

How long do bankruptcies stay on your credit report? A Chapter 7 filing stays on your report for 10 years after the discharge date. It can stay on as a public record for much longer, but it shouldn't be in your report after 10 years has passed. A Chapter 13 filing can appear for seven years after the discharge date.

But that doesn't mean that you can't get a mortgage after a bankruptcy. Far from it. There are lenders who specialize in making mortgage loans to those who have experienced a bankruptcy that has been discharged even one day ago.

Even conventional loans underwritten under Fannie Mae or Freddie Mac guidelines allow mortgages to be approved even if there is a bankruptcy on a credit report. For most conventional loans, the lender wants two to four years to have passed since the discharge date, and also wants to see that the bankruptcy was out of the borrower's control.

Being out of the borrower's control means that it was the result of something like illness, loss of job, or divorce. If a borrower simply borrows too much money, begins to get behind on payments, then decides "what the heck" and files for bankruptcy, lenders don't like that attitude. It makes them a little queasy.

Conventional loans will ask that the bankruptcy have been discharged for four years and credit reestablished in at least three consumer accounts. That means that after a bankruptcy is discharged, it's necessary to establish new credit lines. And pay them on time.

There are companies that specialize in bankruptcy accounts. Soon after someone has had a bankruptcy discharged, he will find new credit card offers in his mailbox. Many of those offers will be for secured cards, although some may not be. But there are indeed various ways to reestablish credit after a bankruptcy, and there are companies out there that are ready to step in and help.

Government loans such as VA and FHA products are more lenient when it comes to lending after a bankruptcy; each suggests that two years pass before a loan is granted, but neither places particular importance on the circumstances of the bankruptcy, as conventional lenders may.

One additional benefit regarding home loans and bankruptcies that the FHA offers involves a Chapter 13 filing. The FHA will allow someone who is still in Chapter 13 to qualify for an FHA loan. If you're currently in Chapter 13, but you've made your payments to the trustee on time each and every month, then you might qualify for FHA financing. The only drawback might be that the trustee assigned to your case by the bankruptcy courts may not approve of your buying a house while you are still in bankruptcy. After all, most FHA loans require a minimum of 3 percent investment on your part. That means that the trustee would want a pretty good explanation for why you're using that 3 percent to buy a house instead of to pay off your creditors.

Fair enough. But the benefits of home ownership can actually help someone get out of Chapter 13 more quickly than someone who continues to rent—especially if rents in the neighborhood are as high as or higher than regular house payments. I'm sure there have been times when a trustee has refused permission for someone to buy a home with little (or no) money down, but I can't recall such an incident.

If the Bankruptcy Was Within Your Control

If, however, your bankruptcy doesn't quite fit the mold of having been completely out of your control, then take heart. There are plenty of loan programs from reputable lenders that cater to those who are currently in bankruptcy, are just out of bankruptcy, or had a bankruptcy discharge less than a couple of years ago.

These loans, offered by subprime lenders, will adjust your interest rate, ask for a higher down payment, or some combination thereof. Some of these programs require that it be more than two years since the discharge, others ask for one year, and still other programs don't care about the discharge date, but do want the bankruptcy to have been discharged—it could have been discharged yesterday.

The length of time since the discharge is included with other underwriting factors in determining the terms of the new mortgage. And while most such programs offer 30-year fixed-rate programs, by far the most popular choice for these loans is a hybrid, usually a 2/28 or 3/27.

Because interest rates on these programs are higher than on conventional loans, the trick is to get into the house with a lower-rate hybrid, while at the same time rebuilding your credit. There are often prepayment penalties on these loans that last for about the same period as the initial hybrid rate. So get into the house, make the payments on time, then refinance into a conventional loan after the two- or three-year period has expired. The first adjustment on a hybrid can be 5 or 6 percent above your start rate, so plan ahead.

Typical hybrid rate adjustments for bankruptcies would be:

7.50%   No bankruptcies in the previous 24 months
8.00%   No bankruptcies in the previous 12 months
8.50%   Bankruptcies may be less than 12 months but must be
        discharged

Notice that the change in interest rate is $1/2$ percent for each 12-month period. This rate variation is typical of those offered by most subprime lenders, although some may vary. Such programs also do not allow for mortgage late payments within that same period.

If there are mortgage late payments during that period, you can expect the interest rate to increase by another $1/2$ percent, and there must have been no more than one mortgage late payment during the previous 12- to 24-month period.

Mortgage lenders may not mind that much if you'd had a bankruptcy, but they don't want to see mortgage late payments anywhere—or, worse, a mortgage that is included in the bankruptcy.

Most people who get into financial straits can keep their home out of a bankruptcy, and many state laws offer considerable consumer protection that allows homeowners to keep their home or otherwise not include the home in any bankruptcy proceedings. After all, you have to have a place to live, right?

Another no-no that is just as serious as including a mortgage in a bankruptcy is a foreclosure. In fact, any mortgage payment that goes beyond 90 days late is in line for a "notice of deficiency," or NOD. The NOD is a legal notice from the mortgage lender that bad stuff is about to happen. When a lender sees that a payment on a property is or was more than 90 days late, it's going to stay away.

Bankruptcies aren't the end of the world. In fact, they can help people start a new world. Sure, the interest rates and terms on subprime loans are not as good as those offered to people with pristine credit, but really they're not that bad. And they help people who have had bankruptcies in their credit past, recent or not, get back into homeownership.

CHAPTER 18

Consumer Credit
Counseling Services

When you get into financial trouble, these ads seem to pop up suddenly out of nowhere. Consumer credit counseling services, or CCCSs, are organizations, some for profit, some not, that help consumers get their financial lives back in order for the purpose of avoiding bankruptcy.

A credit counselor performs a task similar to that of a Chapter 13 bankruptcy trustee: All debts are added up, and the consumer makes payments to the counselor, who then forwards the money to the creditors.

But a credit counselor may also do other things, such as:

Evaluating a consumer's credit profile

Establishing a monthly budget

Renegotiating current debt with creditors

Managing monthly payments to creditors

The first thing a counselor will do is take a step back from your situation and evaluate exactly where you stand from a credit viewpoint. Your credit report will be run, your current balances will be checked against your monthly statements, and the counselor will check for errors and mostly make sure that the road map (your credit report) is telling the true story.

Your total minimum monthly payments are added together, along with your everyday living expenses, such as food, utilities, clothing, and so on. At this point, a monthly budget is established.

Your counselor may also attempt to renegotiate both your current interest rates and the amounts owed. Sometimes a counselor can contact a credit card company, explain your situation, and state that you have contracted with the counselor to help you with your debt and avoid bankruptcy altogether. The theory is that the credit card company would much prefer to get something rather than nothing, so it will reduce the amount owed, reduce the rate, or a combination of both.

Then each month, instead of making monthly payments to your creditors individually, you make one big payment to the counselor, who divvies up the money among the people you owe and pays them their negotiated share.

Credit counselors can vary in quality, so it's necessary for you to do a little homework. You'll want to contact the Better Business Bureau, and also with any regulatory agency that governs consumer complaints in your state, to see if there have been any complaints.

How do counselors make their money? You may be surprised to learn that usually the credit card companies themselves make payments to such organizations on your behalf. It makes sense if you think about how much more the creditor would lose if you filed for a Chapter 7 bankruptcy instead of renegotiating that debt to a more manageable level, which in fact is managed by a third party—the counselor.

Some of these agencies are less than straightforward. Some counselors will ask for money from you up front. In this case, you're making payments on their "profit" in lieu of or in addition to anything the credit card companies might pay. Ask the agency how it makes its money. It should be able to tell you right away. If you get some hemming and hawing about its being a nonprofit agency and so on, then I'd suggest that you continue your search for a reputable counselor.

It's very important to note that lenders view a credit counseling service almost the same way as they do a bankruptcy, as discussed in Chapter 17. If you're with a credit counselor, it will say so in your credit report, and a lender will look at that entry exactly as it would a regular bankruptcy. If a lender has a loan program that requires that a Chapter 13 or Chapter 7 bankruptcy be discharged before making the loan, then it's very likely that your credit counseling will need to be completed with all creditors paid.

If you're deciding between a credit counselor and Chapter 13, you'll notice that they both accomplish the same thing: They rearrange your monthly debt payments to manageable levels and pay everyone back what they're owed, compared to a Chapter 7, which wipes everything out.

Deciding whether to file for bankruptcy or enter credit counseling is serious business. You need legal counsel or someone who is otherwise fluent in the legal aspects of such a decision to help with this.

CHAPTER 19

Bad-Credit Loans—
The World of Subprime Lending

It used to be that if someone had damaged credit, then she was out of luck when it came to home ownership. At best (or at worst), she would find a "hard money" lender with out-of-this-world interest rates whose design was to make the payments so high that she would be unable to make them and the lender could foreclose on the house.

Now, however, things are different. There are other alternatives for people with damaged credit. These are loans that are designed to help people enjoy the benefits of homeownership, while at the same time helping them get back on their financial feet. These loans are called *subprime*.

Subprime loans are more popular than ever, primarily because lenders have come to understand the limits of these loans as well as their benefits. Depending upon which survey you look at, subprime loans make up about 25 percent of all mortgage lending. In fact, some borrowers bypass FHA lending altogether and go straight for a subprime loan. Either the borrower thinks that since he has impaired credit, he wouldn't qualify for an FHA loan, or his loan officer sent him in that direction.

Subprime lending also has its own secondary market, similar to Fannie Mae or Freddie Mac. And this is a good thing. All subprime lenders offer mortgages that are similar, if not exactly the same. If a subprime lender underwrites a loan in accordance with a particular subprime guideline, then that lender can sell that loan to another lender or investor that specializes in subprime mortgage investing.

In fact, subprime lending has become so accepted that Fannie Mae and Freddie Mac, seeing that they've left a lot of lending business to subprime lenders, have gotten into the fray by introducing their own version of subprime loans. So if subprime loans have been "endorsed" by conventional lenders, then what's the matter with them? Actually nothing, if they're explained correctly at the very beginning of the mortgage process and if the borrowers know that a subprime loan should be viewed as a temporary "fix" to get them back into the mortgage world, not a lifetime albatross hanging around their necks.

The biggest mistake most borrowers make is to "approve" or "deny" themselves. The biggest reason for this is that because there is so much information available on the Internet, most consumers begin there. They do some research and find out what makes a "bad" credit score, assume that their credit score too is "bad," and immediately begin looking for subprime loans. Big mistake.

If you think you've got bad credit, let a lender decide that for you. Those late payments you had on your credit cards or on your car loan last year could mean little, if anything, if you've established good credit in other accounts.

You'll be surprised at how a little tweaking can affect a loan approval. If your score is low, say below 620, then try putting more down. A 620 score with 5 percent down might be difficult for many conventional offerings, but might just be the ticket for an FHA loan. If that doesn't quite make it for an FHA loan with 5 percent down, try putting 10 or 15 percent down. High down payment FHA loans are much more forgiving when it comes to loan approval. If you've got some credit issues and FHA loan limits are right for your area, I'd look at a 10 to 15 percent down FHA loan if you have those resources available.

Subprime loans can come in almost any mortgage type, including both fixed-rate and adjustable-rate programs, but most often the subprime loan of choice is the hybrid. Hybrid ARMs provide a lower than market rate for the first few years, then turn into an annual or periodic adjustable-rate loan. Most of the subprime loans I've closed are either the 2/28 or 3/27 version of the hybrid.

The trick with a subprime loan is to understand specifically what these loans are designed for. They're designed to help you get back on your feet and get you into homeownership. With a subprime loan, you'll want to do everything you can to repair your credit and improve your credit score. One of the best ways to improve your score is to make your mortgage payments on time. You do this with a subprime loan.

And since it can take two or three years of responsible credit use to improve a credit rating, if you are approved for a subprime loan, by the time the initial period of the hybrid is completed, your credit should have been reestablished to the point where you can refinance into a lower-rate conventional loan.

Sure, subprime loans come in various flavors, but their rates can be 2 to 4 percent higher, or more, than those on a conventional loan. The trick with subprime loans is to take the hybrid, pay close attention to your credit patterns, and refinance out of the loan when your hybrid adjusts. Subprime ARMs can have some pretty nasty margins, some as high as 5 percent or more. You don't want to have your payment jump from 6.00 to 11.00 percent after the first 36 months. The subprime loan is a Band-aid, not something to be used for the rest of your life. Also, if you plan to refinance, make sure that you are being realistic. You should realize that if a subprime loan is the only type of loan you qualify for at the time of application, then you won't be in a position to refinance in less than two or three years. That's about how long it will take to repair your credit, which is necessary before you can refinance into a fixed rate, conventional mortgage.

Most subprime loans will carry, where allowed, a prepayment penalty as well. If your loan has a prepayment penalty, be it hard or soft, I wouldn't worry about it too much. Most prepayment penalties will coincide with the fixed portion of the hybrid ARM. If you've chosen a 3/27 hybrid, your prepayment penalty period will usually be three years; on a 2/28, it will usually be two years. Most loans of this type also give you the option of "buying out" the prepayment penalty, either in points (usually one year of buyout will cost $1/2$ to 1 point) or by increasing your rate.

If you buy out one year of prepayment penalty, you can anticipate an increase in rate of $1/4$ percent for each year you bought out.

On a side note, it's very important not to pay discount points when using a subprime loan. We'll discuss points and closing costs in great detail in Chapter 24, but if your goal is to refinance in two or three years, then it doesn't make any sense to pay points to get a lower rate—you won't be keeping that subprime mortgage long enough to get the full benefit of the lower rate.

For example, a $300,000 subprime loan may be offered at 7.50 percent for a 2/28 hybrid. That works out to a $2,097 monthly payment. Remember that your goal is to refinance in 24 months after you've repaired your credit. On that same loan, your lender offers to reduce your rate to 7.00 percent if you pay 2 points, or $6,000. That's a common spread.

The monthly payment on $300,000 using 7.00 percent is $1,995. Yes, your monthly payment is now over $100 lower. But you paid $6,000 for that privilege. If you refinance into a conventional loan in 24 months, you will have saved just over $2,400, but you in effect lost $3,600 because you "bought down" the rate.

Lenders offer "zero-point" subprime loans just as they would offer zero-point conventional or FHA loans. If your lender doesn't offer a no-points option on your 2/28 or 3/27 loan, look for another lender. Believe me, there are hundreds out there. Keep your loan costs on a subprime loan low if your goal is to refinance after a short period or right at the end of your hybrid term. The math rarely works out otherwise.

Subprime loans offer more variables than conventional or government loans do. If a conventional loan offers 5.50 percent on a 30-year fixed-rate loan with 10 percent down, most likely that's the rate you'll get if you put 20, 30, or even 40 percent down. But not with subprime loans.

Subprime lending makes allowances as different variables are adjusted. These variables are:

Down payment
Debt ratios
Credit scores

A subprime lender will offer you a better deal if any of those three variables is adjusted—and an even better one if all three are improved.

Let's say that if your credit score is 590, your ratios are at 50, and your minimum down payment is 10 percent, you might get a 2/28 subprime offering of 8.00 percent. But if you put down 20 percent instead of 10 percent, your rate might be reduced by $1/4$ percent.

If you choose to put down more money, say 30 percent, and this also reduces your debt ratios to 44 percent, you'll find that your rate may go down by another percent. Or suppose your ratios are under 50, but your LTV is 69. Again, you'll get a better rate.

Subprime lenders are fairly strict about such guidelines. In these cases, credit scores, LTVs, and debt ratios are in fact set in stone. In subprime lending, your rate in fact goes up by $1/4$ percent if your score is 589 and not 590, or if your debt ratio is 46 percent instead of 45. Unlike conventional lending, which rarely has such rigid requirements, subprime lending doesn't allow for many exceptions.

How can you determine which combination of variables is best for you? That depends. Do you in fact have enough money to make a larger down payment? If you don't, then you'll need to borrow less to keep your ratios down. Or you'll need to find some more income in the form of a new job, another borrower who will live in the house with you, or a raise.

If you do have the resources to choose the combination of variables that can help you most, ask your lender or loan officer. On subprime loans, each lender has a grid that charts the different variables that will affect your rate. If you get the best rate when your ratio is below 45, then put down the precise amount of money that will cause your loan amount to be exactly what it needs to be to keep your ratios in line.

If you're having trouble getting qualified because a ratio is a little high, you may in fact want to explore paying points to get a lower rate. No, it's not the best of all worlds, but in this instance you're simply trying to qualify for your required loan amount, and if you need a lower rate, then you have little choice other than to pay the points to get that lower rate or to explore an ARM with a lower start rate. On average, one discount point will reduce your interest rate by $1/4$ percent.

If you're being quoted something that's nowhere near this ratio, say 2 points for $1/4$ percent, then get a new loan officer.

Conventional loans underwritten under Fannie Mae or Freddie Mac guidelines also have loan programs for people with damaged credit. These loan programs are fixed-rate loans, mostly of the 30-year variety, and are always submitted via an AUS.

If a loan submission doesn't get an approval using Freddie Mac's LP, for example, the notice from LP will tell the lender whether the loan is available under "expanded criteria." Such offerings mean, "No, I can't approve you under the terms submitted, but I do have a counteroffer." The counteroffer is an interest rate that is higher than that under normal credit circumstances.

Unfortunately these "subprime" counteroffers are rarely better than a subprime lender's best rates. In fact, they may be worse if the borrower has less than 20 percent to put down. If a conventional loan has less than a 20 percent down payment, mortgage insurance is required. Add the mortgage insurance to a 30-year fixed rate that is higher than that on many subprime offerings, and it might very well be to your best advantage to use a subprime lender if you have damaged credit.

Let's compare a subprime offering from a subprime lender and a conventional expanded criteria loan for an amount of $200,000 with 5 percent down.

The rate for the conventional expanded criteria loan could be 1.50 percent above a conventional lender's best rates. So if the best conventional rate today is 7.00 percent, then an expanded criteria loan rate would be 8.50 percent—plus mortgage insurance.

The principal and interest payment on a 30-year loan of $200,000 at 8.50 percent is $1,537. Mortgage insurance for a 95 percent LTV 30-year fixed-rate loan is about $115. The monthly payment including mortgage insurance is $1,537 plus $115, or $1,652.

Next, compare a subprime 3/27 hybrid with 5 percent down. Mortgage insurance is not required on subprime loans with down payments of less than 20 percent. A common rate would be about 7.50 percent, making the monthly payment $1,398. That's $253 less than the conventional loan.

But that's hardly a fair comparison, you say? Yes, the 3/27 loan is fixed for only three years, a much shorter period than 30 years. But remember, when you take a subprime, the goal is to correct past credit mistakes and repair your credit, not to get "married" to a bad loan for the rest of your credit life. A similar subprime 30-year loan rate might in fact be closer to 9.00 percent, but if your goal is to get yourself back on track from a credit standpoint, then a hybrid is your best choice.

Finding the Best Subprime Loan

Finding the best subprime loan will take a bit more homework than comparing one conventional loan with another. The biggest obstacle is finding subprime loans in the first place, and the biggest mistake is thinking that subprime lenders are the only lenders that can help you.

The fact is that because subprime loans are underwritten to the same subprime standards from one lender to the next, there really is very little difference, if any, between the subprime loan at Lender A and the subprime loan at Lender B. It's just that through marketing, advertising, and the loan officer's sales pitch, the loan offered by a given subprime lender might seem different. It rarely is. If it is, then that lender has no intention of ever selling the loan. How could it? The loan wasn't underwritten to universal subprime standards.

One note of advice here: There are in fact "special commitments," whereby a subprime lender will negotiate with an investor to originate a certain subclass of mortgages that may have a variance or two in the underwriting guidelines. In these instances, there will in fact be a difference in the loan, but the lender will have already incorporated those variances into either the price of the loan, the rate, or some combination thereof.

If you're calling around trying to find the best deal, and you find a loan program that permits debt ratios 5 percent higher than other lenders permit on the very same loan, then ask that lender if in fact the loan program has been granted any special variances from the investor.

If you ask your loan officer that question directly, you'll get a blank stare or the phone will appear to have gone dead on the other end. The loan officer probably won't know what you're talking about. But ask anyway and have the loan officer find out for you. When a loan officer quotes loan terms that differ from those offered by other institutions, too often the loan officer either is making a mistake or knows in advance he is misquoting the loan terms, intending to take your application money, then change the terms later on down the road. Special commitments aren't uncommon, but they're rarely found in the subprime market. Heck, they're hard to find in any market.

To find the best subprime lender, start by looking at companies that offer standard conventional loans, not ones that specialize in subprime loans. Almost every lender that makes standard loans such as conventional or government ones also offers subprime loans. In fact, most lenders have a subprime division that offers nothing except loans for those who have hurt their credit.

Don't prejudge yourself. The difference between a conventional rate and the rate on a subprime loan could be 2, 3, 4, or even 5 percent. You owe it to yourself to try for the best possible offering right out of the gate.

Get some referrals from Realtors, friends, or neighbors. Or do some research on the Internet. But to start out, work with a name you recognize. This doesn't mean that you won't finally end up with a lender you've never heard of, but working initially with someone that you either have worked with before or were referred to will give that lender a bit more credibility when you are researching subprime loans.

When you call the lender, be up front about your situation. If you think you have bad credit, tell the loan officer not just that you think you have bad credit but, more importantly, why you think your credit is bad. Often the difference between what you think is bad credit and what in the real lending world is really considered subprime can be worlds apart.

Several years ago, when I was just getting into the mortgage business as a mortgage broker in San Diego, a Realtor referred a client to me. I called the client, introduced myself, and began telling her why she should be doing business with my mortgage company. She abruptly stopped me, saying, "I have bad credit, so I'm not going to waste too much of your time."

I informed her that there were lenders who make loans every day to people with damaged credit, but she wouldn't budge. She didn't want to apply for a loan until she knew what the terms would be, but of course I couldn't tell her what the terms would be without seeing a credit report and reviewing her application. Instead, I gave her the "worst-case" scenarios, quoting rates much higher than those advertised in the local newspapers.

Because those rates were higher, she was reluctant to make an offer on a home she really, really wanted to live in, so she waited and waited. She was unable to make a decision even on whether to fill out a loan application or review her credit report, much less make an offer on a house.

A few months passed, and I eventually stopped calling her. Then one day, out of the blue, she placed a call to my office. "Okay," she said. "There's a house I really want to buy, so I guess I'll have to just grin and bear it. I know I have bad credit, so I'd just better take my lumps and move on."

I took her application and ran her credit report. At first, I thought the credit report I was reviewing belonged to someone else. She did have a relatively common name, after all. I called her, told her about the possible mix-up, and asked her if in fact she owned this credit card and that auto payment and so on. She confirmed that those accounts were hers and she had no others. "But where's the bad credit?" I asked her. "It's my car loan. I was late a couple of times, and I'm sure it's on my report." I looked, and, sure enough, there was one late car payment nearly 18 months earlier. Hardly anything for a lender to worry about. I told her that was not a problem, especially since everything else looked so good.

She was skeptical at first, then completely happy when she closed on the house she had really, really wanted. She thought I was some kind of magical loan person who could do wonders. I told her it was no big deal, but she never believed it. She thought she had bad credit, and there was nothing I could do to convince her otherwise.

The good side of the story is that she got what she wanted, but the bad side is that there were lots of other houses that she let slip away simply because she didn't apply. What you should do is find a lender, tell the loan officer exactly why you think you have good, bad, or terrible credit, and let her go to work.

Your loan officer will first input your data into the institution's software program, run your credit report, then submit your application for an AUS decision. Some loan officers forgo the initial credit report because the AUS will pull one of its own. If you don't get your approval on the first run, your loan officer will be able to tell you exactly why when the AUS returns with a decision.

When an AUS doesn't approve a loan, the report will list the reasons why, with the most important reason being listed first. If you can correct the first two issues, or at least improve on them, try for another decision. If you can't correct those items, ask your loan officer to try for a subprime offering.

It's challenging to compare a subprime loan with a conventional one. The subprime loan you're being quoted is usually a different type of loan from the one you initially applied for. One might be a hybrid and one might be fixed, for example. Instead of trying to compare loan types, keep your original goal in your mind while keeping closing costs the same.

The best way to compare loans may not always be the rate; it could also be the acquisition costs, or closing costs, on both loans.

When comparing two types of loans, make sure you're paying the exact amount of discount points and/or origination charges on each. If you were originally quoted a 30-year fixed-rate loan without any points, don't compare that offering with a subprime 3/27 hybrid with 2 points. Instead, get the rate quote on the 3/27 with no points, just like the conventional loan. Only in this way can you truly compare the differences in monthly payments between the two loan types.

After you've gotten your subprime approval and are satisfied that this is the lender's best offering, it's time to shop around a little. Now is the time to call different lenders, even those you've never heard of. Pick up the phone, make some calls, and say, "I've just been preapproved with another lender on a subprime loan. My credit score is XXX, my down payment is X percent, and I've never been in bankruptcy, been more than 30 days late on my rent, . . ."

There's no need to apply all over again, although some lenders or loan officers will require you to. You can always get a general rate quote. If you find some offerings intriguing, then go ahead and make another application. Don't worry about additional credit inquiries affecting your credit score. Remember that the score won't fluctuate if you're applying for the same type of loan at or around the same point in time.

But shop you must, and maybe even especially so with a subprime loan. Loan shopping can get very tricky, and comparing one lender with another and one loan with another can be difficult. Don't think, however, that you're stuck or that you have limited loan choices. There's a great big world out there in subprime lending. Don't be afraid of it. Just understand its place. Subprime loans are a Band-aid, not a lifetime fix.

Beware of Predatory Lending

What is predatory lending? No one really knows exactly. At least, there's no national standard, although certain states have enacted their own legislation trying to determine what is and what is not a predatory loan.

Predatory lending has a nice ring to it. Great sound bite. But defining a predatory loan is really a moving target. What is predatory to one person may be just a subprime loan to another. Technically, a predatory loan is a loan program offered by a lender that tracks down unsuspecting borrowers, then makes mortgage loans to them, hoping that borrowers won't be able to pay back the loans, and so the lender will be able to either refinance the mortgage or foreclose on the home.

Predatory lenders search for people who can't fend for themselves or who don't understand the loan process well enough to determine whether a loan is right for them. For example, a loan officer finds a consumer who is behind on her bills. He does this by buying "leads" from companies that specialize in researching and reporting public information or that advertise in certain places like the Internet or newspapers to attract those with credit or money concerns. "Get rid of all your debt and lower your monthly payments!" or some such. You've seen them.

What happens is a vicious cycle. The loan officer calls the potential customer and gets her to apply for a mortgage. The loan officer pulls the credit report, sees that there is enough equity in the home to pay off the customer's bills, and talks the applicant into taking out the new mortgage.

The new mortgage is higher because it now includes not just the first home loan, but also the credit card balances that the new loan is paying off. Yes, mortgage payments will be lower than credit card payments, but this is where the "predatory" part kicks in.

Now the borrower has new total monthly payments, but because the rate is so high, she begins to feel pinched every month, perhaps even charging everyday items on those very same credit cards that she paid off—but never cancelled.

Soon, the mortgage payments fall into arrears, so the lender calls up the borrower and warns her that if she doesn't get caught up on her home loan, the institution will foreclose. So of course the borrower takes out another loan, with a higher rate, more points, and more money for the lender. Loans can be very, very confusing at best. Throw in terms like "hybrid ARMs" and "negative amortization" and they can be a nightmare. Especially if the borrower pays little attention to such terms, but instead looks only at the lower monthly payment or is facing the prospect of losing her home.

This can happen a couple of times, until finally there is no more equity in the house. The borrower can't make the payments; the lender has made three or four different loans on the same house, with each subsequent loan being larger than the previous one; and finally the borrower loses her home, her credit, and her self-regard. She's lost everything she had. She's been the victim of a predatory lender.

If you think a loan is predatory, it just might be. Every state has a "smell test" that attempts to identify a predatory loan. Be warned, though: What may be considered predatory in one state is not in another. Some states will determine that a loan is predatory if the interest rate exceeds a certain number—say, 10 percent. That would be fine if rates stayed the same all the time, but they don't. Everyone who's been in the business for a while can remember when interest rates were in the high teens. And those rates were reserved for people with good credit!

Just as inflation can affect interest rates, so can market forces such as a recession or a runaway economy. Legislatures that attempt to define what a predatory loan is and is not by identifying a fixed benchmark are making a mistake. While 10 percent may be predatory today, it wasn't 10 to 15 years ago and it may not be 3 or 4 years from now.

Other states define a predatory loan by taking a universal money benchmark and adding a margin to it. A common benchmark is the 1-year Treasury bill. A loan might be considered predatory if the index plus the margin exceeds allowable limits. Some states consider a loan to be predatory if the index plus the margin is 5.00 percent above the index.

Other states adopt limits established by the Home Owners Equity Protection Act, or HOEPA (HOPE-uh), which was most recently modified in 2002. The 2002 modifications to HOEPA declared that any rate more than 8.00 percent above the 1-year Treasury was a HOEPA violation. As one can easily tell, defining a predatory loan is difficult. That's why if the loan you're considering seems predatory, then it just might be.

First, ask yourself if you feel that you are being rushed or hurried into taking a particular loan. Is the loan officer calling you incessantly and warning you that this "offer" will be taken off the table if you don't sign your new loan papers immediately? Is the loan officer warning of potential foreclosure or other bad things that will happen to you if you don't take this loan?

If a loan officer is making you feel weird, something's going on. So do two things: Simply back away and make sure you understand exactly what you're getting into, and compare the loan offering with those of other lenders.

That's right. Slow down. If a crooked loan officer is rushing you to the closing table and saying things like "sign here" and "hurry," then

you have to wonder what's going on. Ask the loan officer why he is push-
ing you so hard. Ask the loan officer if this is a predatory loan.

Loan officers who push predatory loans know what they're doing.
You might find a loan officer who will accidentally exceed a predatory
limit, but if so, she will quickly correct it. Ask the loan officer straight
out, "Pardon me, but is this loan considered predatory by state law or by
HOEPA?" If the loan is in fact predatory, I'll guarantee you that you
won't be contacted by that person again. If that's the case, turn over
copies of all your loan quotes to the state regulating authority and have
the lender busted.

Next, compare loans. By comparing loans from one lender to the
next, you'll be able to tell if one loan has exorbitant fees and another does
not. This works only if you're comparing loans of the exact same type, so
don't trip yourself up that way, either.

Finally, simply refuse to pay outrageous fees. What's outrageous? In
my opinion, anything that exceeds 3 points is too high, as is any origination charge that exceeds 1 percent of the loan amount. There is no requirement that any loan have a certain amount of points added to the
cost that does not subsequently reduce your interest rate.

Another expensive item found on most predatory loans is credit insurance. This is an insurance policy that, should you die, will pay off
your mortgage. While this might be a useful option in a few instances, if
it's a requirement for your loan—according to your loan officer, anyway—then you're a victim of a predatory lender. If you're getting gouged
by closing costs, then don't take the loan.

I want to bring up another controversial item called the *yield spread
premium*. A yield spread premium, or YSP, is an amount of money expressed as a percentage of the loan amount you're borrowing.

The yield spread is the difference between one interest rate and another. If a $100,000 loan is available at 7.00 percent with 1 point or 7.25
percent with zero points, then the yield spread is 1 percent of $100,000,
or $1,000.

A yield spread *premium* is the difference between a one-point loan
and a zero-point loan at a higher rate. It's usually the lender that gets the
difference. For example, if 7.00 percent is available at 1 point and 7.25

percent at zero points, then the loan officer might instead quote you 7.50 percent at zero points. You get the same zero-point loan, but you also got a higher interest rate. The difference is that the loan officer just made more money off of you.

YSPs have been around for a long time; they've just been called different things. When I was a mortgage broker in the late 1980s and early 1990s, the YSP was called a "rebate." As a broker, I could quote a borrower a zero-point rate of 8.00 percent. But also as a broker, I could choose which lender I wanted to send that loan to. It wouldn't make any difference which lender I selected as long as the borrower got what he wanted and what he was originally offered. I would compare the pricing offered by three or more different lenders and would determine who would pay me the most money if I sent the loan there. Lender A might quote me 1.25 points in rebate, Lender B might quote me 1.375 points in rebate, while finally Lender C, who was aggressively pursuing the mortgage broker market, might price an 8.00 percent interest rate at 1.50 points in rebate.

On a $200,000 loan, there's a difference of $^{1}/_{2}$ a discount point between Lender A and Lender C. That's $1,000 in revenue. I would choose Lender C and make a little more money on the loan, while the borrower still got the rate he wanted at the very same price—zero points.

That's what a YSP is. Are YSPs bad things? No, I don't think so. If you use a mortgage broker and demand a no-points, no-origination-fee loan, then how do you expect the broker to make any money? She won't do the loan for free; why would she? She makes her money through the YSP paid by the lender. Can YSPs be a bad thing? Sure they can, just like most facets of mortgage lending when they're abused. But they're not a bad thing on their face.

Predatory lending practices have been around for a long, long time, and it seems like every time a law is passed to help consumers fight predatory lending, a new way to screw the consumer rears its ugly head. Predatory lending will always be a consumer issue, but the best way to attack it is to question every charge, shop around for your home loan, and refuse to be a victim.

CHAPTER 21

Should You Just Wait?

That's a fair question—and something that you should consider carefully. Are you ready to buy a home? Will you be worse off than before? Buying a house is no small decision—if you don't like the house after all, you can't just walk away. Interest rates on subprime loans are higher than those on conventional or government fare, so does it make sense to not use a subprime loan, but wait to repair your credit instead? Here are a few things to consider.

How much higher is your monthly payment with a subprime loan when compared to a conventional product?

One thing about subprime mortgage rates is that in reality, while they're higher than what's offered those with the best credit, they're really a bargain when compared to other types of lending.

Consider someone with excellent credit who gets a credit card. Maybe that person gets a rate of, say, 8.00 percent. But compare that rate with one offered to someone who doesn't have great credit. For people who have had late payments on their credit cards, "subprime" interest rates can be higher than that 8.00 percent—much higher. In fact, credit card rates can be 25, 26, or 28 percent. That's stratospheric when compared to the differences in mortgage rates.

Compare a $300,000 30-year loan at 8.00 percent with one at 28 percent. The 30-year fixed-rate payment at 8.00 percent is $2,201. The payment at 28 percent? How about a whopping $7,001 each and every month. Try choking down that mortgage payment. What irks me about this is that you don't hear consumer groups yelling and screaming about the nosebleed interest rates charged by credit card companies the way they scream each and every day about predatory lending.

Interest rates on mortgages for those with excellent and those with damaged credit will differ, but really by just a few percentage points. If conventional financing on a 30-year fixed-rate loan is available at 6.00 percent, then someone with collection accounts and judgments might find a subprime offering at 8 to 9 percent. That's nowhere near the 18 to 20 percent differences found in credit card and automobile lending.

Sure, subprime rates are higher, but not that much by any standard. If you can handle the higher monthly payments with a subprime mortgage compared to a conventional one, then there is no reason to wait.

If, however, your debt ratios with a subprime loan do indeed make you sweat when you write a check for the mortgage payment each month, then you might want to wait a few months to get some old bills paid off or find some new income somewhere—or buy a less expensive home.

If you do buy a house using a subprime lender, it's extremely important that you begin fixing your credit right away. Typically your best option for a subprime loan is a hybrid because your initial rate will be lower than what's offered with a fixed-rate loan. But beware: After the initial adjustment period, your rate can go up significantly compared to what you previously were paying. If you're not confident that your credit will be improved in time to refinance after two or three years, then you should in fact either wait until your credit is improved or take the fixed rate.

Look at the numbers for renting compared to buying. As mentioned in the early chapters of this book, evaluating a rent-versus-buy strategy is key. For those with excellent credit and strong debt ratios, buying rather than renting is usually an easy decision. There are simply too many advantages of home ownership.

With subprime lending, you'll need to scrutinize the transaction a little more closely. Sit down with a pencil and paper and calculate the differences over the next 24 months to see whether you should wait for your credit to improve or buy right now.

For example, suppose there is a $200,000 house that you want to buy and you have 10 percent down. Assume a conventional mortgage at 6.00 percent, a subprime 2/28 loan at 8.00 percent, and rent for a similar house at $1,500 per month.

Conventional monthly payment (includes $80 per month mortgage insurance) at 6.00 percent	$1,279 per month
Subprime monthly payment (no mortgage insurance required) at 8.00 percent	$1,394 per month
Rent	$1,500 per month

The difference between the conventional loan and the subprime loan over the next 24 months is $2,760. The difference between the subprime loan and renting is $2,544. In this example, it makes sense to buy now rather than rent because your house payments are lower than rent.

Note that these examples show principal and interest only, and do not include homeowner's insurance and property taxes. Assuming an annual insurance bill of $900 and property taxes of $2,000, you'll need to add another $241 to the monthly totals in order to get a cash flow difference. Now when you add the taxes and insurance, the cost is actually higher with a subprime loan: $1,394 + $ 241 = $1,635 compared to renting at $1,500.

The difference between renting and a conventional loan payment at $1,279 + $241 = $1,520 is only $20. But in this example it's still better to buy, as there are property tax and mortgage interest tax deductions that are not available to renters. So it makes sense to go ahead and buy now.

Even given the differences between the conventional and subprime loans, there is still a sizable advantage to buying and owning compared to renting.

But the key here is to make absolutely certain that the things that got your credit in bad shape in the first place stop, and stop now. If you're over the top or feel pinched every month, then don't buy. Wait until you feel better about your situation. But waiting because conventional rates are better than subprime loans by a couple of percentage points is usually not worth it.

The advantages of home ownership compared to renting, even with a subprime loan, may still make buying most often your better choice.

CHAPTER 22

Buying Foreclosures

$\mathbf{B}$uying foreclosures is a whole new world of real estate. There are investors who do nothing but track down homes that are about to go into foreclosure or find homes that have already been foreclosed upon, hoping to strike the ultimate real estate deal. Buying foreclosed properties doesn't mean that you're going to get to move into a house for free and all you need to do is take up the payments. While that option may have been around several years ago, days when nonqualifying assumable mortgages on foreclosed property were available at half their value are long gone.

Why Do Lenders Foreclose?

First, either the lender made a big mistake or something really bad happened to the borrowers. The lender made a loan on a home that didn't "perform," and now the lender is forced to recover its asset. And this is no easy task. In America, we treat property ownership, especially ownership of our home and our land, as sacred. In no other place on earth will you find such a distinction as to homeownership. Part of being American is owning your very own home. That's an American dream.

This means that consumers are given every protection imaginable to help them keep their property, with some states being more vigorous than others.

When a lender forecloses on a property, it's a last resort. The borrowers simply could no longer pay the mortgage, and the lender was forced to recover the home. A lender usually loses money in a foreclosure, especially if the property was bought with little or no down payment.

Foreclosures occur when something bad happens to the borrowers. No one buys a home with the intention of having it taken away from them. Foreclosure destroys credit and ruins families. A home is usually the last thing someone gives up when he falls behind on his bills. He'll allow his autos to be repossessed or accounts to go into collection before he'll give up his home.

When a home goes into foreclosure, the borrower is typically more than three months behind in mortgage payments. More than three months have passed with no money being paid on the property. The lender gives formal notice to foreclose on the home, with the actual method varying from state to state. That formal notice is called a *lis pendens*, which means "pending lawsuit." Or a notice of default, or NOD, may be recorded right after the 90 + -day period has elapsed. Since this is a public, legal recording, this is where the initial information that a home is about to go into foreclosure comes from. You as an individual can pore over public records to look for new lis pendens filings, or you can find a company that does this for a living.

The lender has lost at least three months' worth of interest, plus the other months' interest that it would have gotten had the consumers continued to pay on the house. There may also be back property taxes that haven't been paid, and lawyers—lots of those—plus any real estate commissions the lender has to pay should it use a Realtor to find a buyer for the home.

After all the expenses are subtracted, lenders may typically get only $0.50 on the dollar. You can see that if a lender has more than a few of those, it won't be a lender very long. That's also why lenders scrutinize borrowers so carefully during the approval process. Foreclosure is the last thing they want.

When a bank takes back a property, it becomes real estate owned, or REO. Almost every lender or bank has an REO department. Some lenders have people, usually Realtors, who are assigned to market these homes and find buyers.

The theory is that since lenders have already lost a ton of money on these properties and aren't making any more, they'll be willing to sell the property cheap and fast to stop the bleeding. And mostly that's correct. But simply contacting an REO department at a bank doesn't mean you'll get an investment bonanza.

The bank will have a minimum that it will sell REOs for, and it will market them just like any other house. Bank REO departments are also easier to work with than other types of foreclosure buying, such as sheriff's auctions or tax sales. This means you just make an offer on a home, it gets accepted, and you buy it. With auctions, which can lead to "bidding wars" right on the courthouse steps, there may also be other factors involved, such as possible previous liens or unseen damage.

There are real estate companies that specialize in working with REO departments. There are also Realtors who specialize in finding and marketing REOs. Banks and other lenders will typically have a working contract with a real estate company to market and sell their REOs.

Most REO departments will make sure that the property is in good order, that physically the property is in good enough shape for a lender to lend on it, and that there are no current or previous claims of ownership, with this covered by a title insurance policy.

When you buy an REO, unless you're paying cash, you'll need to get a mortgage. REOs aren't special in the sense that you can simply walk into a home and start making house payments. Most REOs don't have assumable loans on them, and even the ones that do make you qualify for the assumption just as if you were getting a new loan.

The advantage with buying REOs is that you just might find a heck of a deal. You want to buy a $500,000 home for $50,000? Good luck. Just because a house has been taken back by a lender doesn't mean that the lender is going to make another mistake and give away $450,000 in equity. But the bank has usually set a price that it is willing to accept rather than simply trying to get as much money as possible.

A misconception about REOs, and foreclosures in general, is that the equity in the property (the value minus any secured note) is automatically awarded to the buyer. It may well be, once the property is yours. But you can't use that assumed equity as any part of your down payment if you're going to get financing.

For instance, suppose a home is valued at $300,000 by an appraiser, but the bank is willing to sell it to you for $250,000. Your lender will determine your loan basis using the $250,000 amount, not the $300,000. If you're going to be taking out a loan that requires a down payment, you'll need to qualify for that loan at a $250,000 sales price just as if the home weren't an REO.

What do banks typically charge for an REO? For starters, they try to get their money back, but that's more than just the outstanding loan balance. A lender will add up what's owed it plus any costs incurred because of foreclosure. For example, to determine a minimum selling price on a foreclosed home, the lender will start with the outstanding loan balance.

Outstanding loan balance	$ 150,000
Interest in arrears (past due payments)	$ 10,000
Back property taxes due	$ 3,000
Attorney and legal fees	$ 5,000
Real estate commissions	$ 5,000
Minimum amount to sell (total)	$ 173,000

The lender will set a minimum sales price of $173,000, then take that number and compare it to the prices of other similar houses in the foreclosed property's neighborhood. If homes in that neighborhood are selling for $300,000, then the lender will try to get as close to that figure as possible. If however, the bank is simply getting tired of keeping the property (banks do get very tired of it, quite frankly), it'll price it to sell as quickly as possible, while at the same time getting a good return.

Lenders don't like to be in the real estate business; that's why they use a Realtor to help them sell the property and determine the "trigger price" of the home: the exact price that will both sell the home as fast as possible and yield the greatest return to the lender within that period.

How do you find REOs? There are specialists who can find them for you, but you can also do a lot of the legwork yourself by simply making a few phone calls or e-mails to the bank or lending institution. If you call any lender on the phone and ask for its REO department, it'll know what you're talking about.

Some lenders keep a list of their REOs. Depending upon the size of the lender or bank, there may be an entire REO department that will negotiate directly with you or your agent, or it may simply use a local Realtor or two that have agreed to market the bank's homes at a negotiated fee. While some Realtors might charge 6 percent as a standard commission, a Realtor might negotiate to get all the bank's REO listings and sell the homes at a discount. Whatever the size of the lender, it will have methods for getting rid of property that has been recovered from defaulting borrowers.

The absolute best way to find REOs is to employ a buyer's agent. A buyer's agent is a Realtor who acts simultaneously as your agent and your negotiator. The best part about this is that the buyer's agent doesn't cost you anything. It's the seller of the property who pays your agent, not you.

When using a buyer's agent to find REOs, you want a Realtor who has experience in these markets, not simply experience at negotiating the price of a home. A buyer's agent should have experience with the lender you're working with; that way, the agent may have an idea of what the lender is willing to accept as a sales price. Using a buyer's agent will also give you the upper hand when it comes to establishing a true market value for the home you want to buy by researching recent similar sales in your area.

If you can buy a $500,000 home from a lender's REO department for $400,000, wouldn't you like to know that? You can if you use an experienced Realtor who knows the neighborhood, the lender, and the current real estate market. If you can find such a person and you're ready to get into the foreclosure area, there is no other way to go. Expert advice and it costs you nothing? Where else can you find such a deal?

Sheriff's Sales and Auctions

Depending upon where you live, homes can be auctioned off to the highest bidder to satisfy previous debts. These debts can be from mortgages gone bad, judgments against the property (where allowed), or back property or income taxes. For all practical purposes, a sheriff's sale and an auction are generally one and the same.

In areas where they're called sheriff's sales, they're called this because the county or parish seat is at the courthouse, where public records are stored. The auction will usually take place on the steps of the courthouse.

You can do all sorts of research on buying foreclosures and how to win public auctions, but if you're a rookie at this, be forewarned: There are professional investors who do nothing except research, buy, and sell foreclosures. You can do the same, but you need to know the basics of buying homes at an auction.

First, the property may or not be occupied. The occupant may be the current owner who is being foreclosed upon, or it may be a renter who may or may not have any clue whatsoever that anything is going on with the property she's renting.

One thing to note is that at an auction, you buy the house "as is." This means that you may not necessarily be able to get an inspection or appraisal of the property. This is a big difference between buying an REO and buying at an auction. You won't know about any defects or maintenance issues. But you can, in fact, anticipate that if the current owner is behind on his bills, he may also be behind on standard maintenance.

A hot water heater can cost a thousand dollars or more. If a homeowner can't afford to make the house payments, then if there's a problem with the hot water heater, do you think she's fixed or replaced it? Are there some plumbing issues? Maybe there's been a water leak in the house, but because you can't get inside it, there's no way for you to find out.

But then again, you might have the opportunity to check out the home. First, why not call the owner? Tell him that you're thinking of buying his home, and would he have a few minutes to talk about the shape of the house itself. Is everything in order? Is there anything that needs to be fixed? Don't get your feelings hurt if the owner isn't all that cooperative; after all, he's losing his house. But if you're getting ready to make a bid on a home, you need to do what you can to find out the condition of the home.

Or, you may find that there are renters there. You can ask them the same questions, and they might be a bit more talkative than an owner. Usually a renter is first in line when telling about things that are wrong with the house; after all, she is paying rent, so she should get a home that's in good working order.

You can also do a little research on your own by investigating county records either in person or, hopefully, online if your appraisal or taxing district has posted all its information. Such information will include not only the name and numbers of the owner, but when the property was built, the approximate square footage, and the most recent year's appraised value. If there are taxes in arrears, you'll find that information there as well.

But remember, you're not a professional at this game; there are others who do this all day long. When a lis pendens is filed, the homeowner may suddenly find letters in her mailbox wanting to "help" by buying the property before the foreclosure takes place. This, of course, not only keeps the house out of foreclosure and keeps that negative off the owner's credit report, but also stops the auction and sale process altogether.

If you really want to buy a property, it might help that you're not a professional trying to take advantage of a negative situation, but rather an individual who wants to buy the home. Some people look for foreclosures in order to make a quick profit, while others are looking for a new place to live.

How does a real estate auction work? Mostly like any other, really. There'll be an announcement of the inventory of homes to be auctioned off, where the auction will be held, and at what time. Many counties have set times every month or every quarter when they auction off real estate, but whichever method is used, the auction procedure is typically the same. When a home is auctioned off, the lender will typically have a minimum sales price it is willing to accept. If that price isn't met, the lender will take the home off the market and go back to square one.

When you go to an auction, there will be a starting price, then the bidding begins. If this is your first auction, be prepared. There are professionals here who know what they're willing to pay and what they're not. They don't let auction fever get hold of them, so that they lose their financial head. If a property gets too pricey, in their opinion, they don't buy, but simply wait for the next one. If you have a particular property in mind that you know is coming up for auction, make sure you've done your homework.

Check out the condition of the property as best you can by talking with the owner or tenants, get a professional inspection done if possible, and look at other homes in the area that have recently sold. Stay within your pre-set bidding limits. Don't let a bargain turn into an overpriced albatross.

To make a bid, you simply raise your hand, and when the bidding is over, it's over. Let's say you won the bidding on a $400,000 house and got it for $300,000. The sheriff will say, "Congratulations on your bid; now, where's your money?"

Many auctions will let you give a deposit, usually a minimum of 10 percent of the winning bid price, in the form of a cashier's check. You will then typically have less than 24 hours to come up with the difference. You've made a commitment to buy; you can't back out if you simply change your mind. These auctions are serious business with no room for a change of heart.

If you're going to get a mortgage, you'll apply just as you would with any other purchase. There's not much time to get everything completed—an appraisal, title search, home inspection, and so on—so it's best to get preapproval for a mortgage loan before you ever reach the courthouse steps. In this way, you'll be prepared to close in short order and will be able to get a cashier's check quickly.

But this is a bad time to find out that there's a problem with the furnace that will cost $10,000 to repair. Or that the home has settled and needs some foundation work. The home was auctioned off as is, and you won the auction, so now you have to pay. A lender won't make a loan on a home if it has significant structural problems.

The need for foundation repairs will stop a home loan application dead in its tracks. A lender will want the foundation fixed and certified as repaired before the loan will move forward. Even if you've been preapproved before the auction, if there's a problem with the property, there'll be a big problem with the loan.

If there's a problem with your loan, the sheriff doesn't care. You won the auction; now pay up. If the auction allows you to have a certain period after the auction to have the property inspected, then you'll have an opportunity to back out of the agreement, but you may not get your $30,000 back.

Some auctions aren't so lenient and won't let you pay 10 percent down. Instead, they're tough—so tough that they make you write a check right then and there. Oh, and make that a cashier's check. They'll give you some time to go to the bank and get that arranged, thank you.

Your best bet is most likely to avoid any auctions. That is, unless you really decide to get into that business. If that's the case, you need to do more state-specific research than this book can provide. But if you have the stamina for it and can do the necessary research, you just might find the bargain of a lifetime.

Finding the Best Deal

Whether you're buying a home with no money down, have impaired credit, or have income that is hard to prove, it comes down to this: finding the best deal. After all, even with all the work you've done up to this point to find the right program that fits your needs, you still have to do your share of shopping. If you don't get the best deal you can, you'll be paying for that mistake on the first of every month when you write your house payment check. To get the best deal, you have to find both the best lender and the best loan officer who can find you the best rate and terms available for your situation.

The most difficult thing to do when trying to find the best deal is to hold your ground. By that I mean that it's absolutely critical that you don't change the type of loan program you're looking for in the middle of the process.

When a loan officer or a lender can't compete on a particular loan program that day, you can expect her to try to provide an alternative. Mortgage lending is just like any other business. Say you go to the mall for a pair of sneakers. You already know your brand, your size, and the color you want. The first store you go into offers the sneakers for $100. The next store offers the same pair of sneakers for $110. Where are you going to buy those sneakers?

The higher-priced sneaker salesman knows that his sneakers are more expensive, so he has a plan. This plan is to steer you into another brand of sneakers that he may be more competitive on. Do you think this doesn't happen in the mortgage business? Of course it does. It's easy to get sidetracked.

If your situation requires a zero-money-down conventional loan, then start your shopping there and don't change. If you do change programs and find that another program will work better for you, then make absolutely certain that you give all the other lenders the opportunity to give you a quote on that new loan program. Don't let a lender switch on you.

In finding the best deal, once you've determined which loan program you're going to stick with, you next need to find the best lender, right? How do you do that? You get some referrals.

Start with someone you know or have a relationship with. This might very well be your bank down the street, or maybe a mortgage company you've worked with before. You may not end up with either of these, but at least you now have a cornerstone on which to build your search.

Next, get referrals from professionals in the business. Get some referrals from your Realtor; he probably knows every retail lender in the neighborhood. Lenders employ loan officers who can bring in mortgage business. Most successful loan officers have built steady relationships with Realtors, who refer clients to them every day. And get more than one referral; ask your Realtor for two or three lenders you can talk with.

At this stage, identify the types of companies you've been referred to. You know your bank and you may know another mortgage company, but sit down in front of your computer and start Googling everyone.

Visit each company's web site and determine if it's a mortgage broker or a mortgage banker. On the web site, usually in the "About Us" section, you'll be able to tell which type of lending company this is. If you're looking for a mortgage banker that works primarily with correspondent lenders, the only way you'll find out if that's the type of banker you're dealing with is to call the lender up and ask.

When you do, don't be surprised by the alarm you may sense from the person answering your question. She's not used to being asked that question, and when someone does ask it, she knows that she's dealing with an educated consumer.

Next, you'll want to contact the state regulatory agency responsible for enforcing licensing and handling consumer complaints. This is also available on the lender's web site, usually something to the effect of "ABC Mortgage is a Licensed Mortgage Broker # 123456 and regulated by the Department of Mortgages" or some agency.

State regulation of bankers and brokers varies from state to state. The regulations seem to change each time a new legislature convenes, but it's easy to find the proper authorities. If you find the proper regulatory agency, you can contact it to see if there have been any complaints, fines, or punishment involving the mortgage operation. Also contact the Better Business Bureau to see if the operation has made people mad.

Any business can tell you that while it's made people mad at it on more than one occasion, this has usually been the result of an honest mistake or a communication issue. It's possible that a consumer complaint means nothing more than a disgruntled customer who didn't get the price he wanted on an automobile, so be fair here.

If, on the other hand, you see a series of violations or complaints, or, worse yet, criminal or civil suits, filings, or judgments, then you've done all the homework you need to on that mortgage company—stay away from it.

Once you've identified a company that you might want to do business with, it's time to contact the loan officer you've been referred to. When you get a referral from a Realtor who has been around the block a few times, you can pretty much trust that referral. Why? If a loan officer makes a Realtor look bad or otherwise screws up a deal, you can bet that that Realtor won't refer people to that loan officer again. Forget the commissions the Realtor lost; it's her integrity that's at stake. Bad loan officers don't do business with good real estate agents.

At this point, you've narrowed your search to two or three mortgage companies. But no matter how much you've researched the operation, it's really the loan officer who makes or breaks its reputation. A mortgage lender can have the biggest advertising budget in the world, but every bit of that money can go down the drain with just one lousy loan officer. I've known some absolutely terrible loan officers who worked for mortgage companies that absolutely everyone has heard of. I also personally know

of some top-notch loan officers who work for companies you've absolutely never, ever heard of.

It's not the company that gets you your best deal—it's the loan
officer.

Now it's time to crunch a few numbers. Now it's time to begin negotiating. Now it's time to pit your chosen loan officers against each other
to compete for your business.

Now you're seeing how much commission the loan officer is going
to give up in order to get your deal.

Most loan officers are paid on commission—at least, the successful
ones are. Loan officers who have been in the business for several years
and get loans referred to them typically make $300,000 to $400,000 per
year. Loan officers who do 10 or 20 deals per month make good money.
One of my former loan officers who still works in San Diego is a million-
aire. So is his boss.

Since different lenders offer basically the same mortgages at about
the same price and you've narrowed down your choices to two loan officers, what else is there to negotiate besides how much money the mortgage company is willing to make on your particular deal?

Let's say you have a $300,000 deal waiting to close; you can assume
that the mortgage company is making anywhere from $3,000 to $6,000
on your loan if it can close it for you. Most loan officers will split that
income with their company, resulting in their commission. In your case,
each loan officer could make $3,000 from placing your mortgage.

The next consideration is getting your rate quote. Mortgage rates can
change throughout the day, so a rate quote on Tuesday may be significantly higher or lower than a quote on Thursday. If you read interest-rate
quotes in your Sunday paper, those rates are already several days old,
plus they may not be available by the time your mortgage company opens
up on Monday morning.

To make sure you're comparing apples to apples and providing an
even playing field for your loan officers to compete on, you must get your
rate quotes on the same exact day, hopefully within just a few minutes
of one another. Most lenders don't issue their mortgage rates until well
after the markets open, but most rates are available by 11:00 EST each

morning. If you call every day at 8:30, you'll get rates from the day before, and a lender typically can't guarantee those rates. They were gone when the markets closed the previous day.

You also need to get your rate quotes covering the exact same period. If you're closing your purchase within 30 days, make sure that your rate quote covers 30 days. Don't assume that the rate quoted to you is good for anything beyond a 10-day period. Some lenders won't discuss interest rates without having received a loan application. To keep everything fair, you need to get rate quotes on the same day, at the same time, for the exact same time period.

Finally, determine if you do or don't want to pay *discount points*. Discount points, or points, are a form of prepaid interest given to the lender in advance in return for a lower interest rate; 1 point equals 1 percent of the loan amount you're borrowing, and 1 point typically buys down your interest rate by $1/4$ percent (2 points by as much as $1/2$ percent). You can run the numbers yourself to see if paying points is worth it or not, and it's easy to do.

Using a 30-year fixed-rate loan at 6.00 percent on a loan amount of $300,000, the monthly payment is $1,798. If you decide to pay 1 point and get a rate of 5.75 percent, then your monthly payment drops to $1,750. The difference, of course, is how much money you paid for that privilege. You paid $3,000 to drop your payment by $48 per month. If you divide $3,000 by $48, that will tell you how many months you need to "recover" that point. In this example, it will take 62.5 months. Not a bad return, but that $3,000 might have been better invested in a mutual fund somewhere.

To get a fair quote, determine ahead of time whether or not you're going to pay points. When you decide, get a rate quote associated with that number of points.

You say; "Please quote me today's rates that are good through the end of the month on a $300,000 loan amount, 30-year fixed with zero points."

If Lender A quotes 7.00 percent with zero points and Lender B quotes 7.125 percent with zero points, you've won. That's how to get a rate quote. If you open it up to all sorts of parameters, such as more points, fewer points, and so on, it's too confusing and too easy for a loan officer to manipulate.

You don't have to get quotes on full points, either. You can get $^1\!/_2$ point or $^3\!/_4$ point. You can also get a rate quote by specifying a particular rate and asking how many points are required to get that rate. By isolating a single variable in the rate quote game, you can be assured of finding the best deal.

But there's one more thing: lender or broker fees. We'll discuss closing costs in more detail in the next chapter, but closing costs can muddy the interest-rate quote waters considerably. You need to know how the game is played. And yes, it is a game—a game using real money, but a game nonetheless.

Lender A might have the best rate at 7.00 percent with no points and Lender B might have 7.125 percent with no points, but Lender B may still have the better offering. How's that? Easy. Junk fees.

Junk fees are charges that lenders make to either help offset other overhead, simply make a little more money, or some combination thereof. Lender A might have a lower rate, but Lender A may have forgotten to tell you about the 1 percent origination fee, the $500 processing fee, the $400 administration fee—and, of course, who can forget the $400 documentation fee? In this example, those fees add up to $4,300, while Lender B had none of those fees. So how do you fix that little problem? By understanding another number, the annual percentage rate, or APR.

The APR is correctly defined as the cost of money borrowed, expressed as an annual rate. If a lender charges you extra costs associated with its loan, those costs must be figured into the total loan cost, expressed in a percentage rate. When $4,300 is added to the $300,000 loan from Lender A, the APR works out to 7.143 percent—higher, albeit only slightly, than the 7.125 percent rate quote from Lender B. There's not much difference in payment, but you also have to pay $4,300 for the privilege of working with Lender A.

Not worth it, is it? The APR is used to isolate any closing costs charged by the lender so that the consumer can get a clearer picture of which lender offers the better deal. A common problem with the APR is the variances you'll see in calculating that number. Worse still, many loan officers have no clue as to its meaning or its utility. If you find that someone doesn't understand or can't interpret the APR number, that's okay as long as you understand it.

In this case, get the lender charges from Lender A and from Lender B and add them up. Once you've determined which has the lower rate with fees accounted for in relation to the lowest fees, you've just found the best deal in the land. Hard work, granted. But this is your mortgage, and you'll be paying it every month. You earn every last dollar you save.

Interest Rates and How They're Set

Maybe the single most misunderstood part of the home loan process is interest rates. Tell me if you've heard this before: "Your mortgage rate should go up tomorrow because the Feds raised the rates today" or "The 30 year Treasury bond rose in price today, so your rates will drop." Forget everything you've heard about who sets what rate. You're about to learn it all right here.

The main reason mortgage rates are mostly the same from lender to lender is that they're all tied to the very same index. For example, 30-year fixed rates are tied to whatever 30-year fixed rates are tied to. The same with 15-year fixed rates. VA 30-year rates are tied to a VA 30-year index. No one lender has a corner on the fixed-rate market—that's why one lender can't offer 4.00 percent when another is offering 6.00 percent on the exact same loan type.

Be wary of advertised rates that are much lower than anyone else's. It simply can't happen. Okay, I guess it can happen, but the lender won't be in business for very much longer if it takes a huge loss every time it issues a loan. I know it's tempting to contact companies you've never heard of that you've found over the Internet or from perusing the papers that offer a super-low rate. But don't bother.

Companies that advertise interest rates well below their competitors are nothing more than "lead" companies or are using bald-faced bait-and-switch tactics. There's a big business in providing mortgage leads to mortgage companies. There are firms that do nothing but attract borrowers in order to sell their information to a home loan company. In fact, the biggest share of online leads consists of those borrowers who have damaged credit.

Lenders can't offer something at a price that's drastically lower than the price offered by other lenders. It can't happen, regardless of whether you found the firm on the Internet or not.

Rates are tied to the rates on various mortgage-backed securities, or mortgage bonds. A common mortgage bond is the Fannie Mae 30-day coupon, which is the index for many 30-year fixed-rate conventional mortgages. There are several other bonds that fix the other indexes that mortgage companies price their loans to.

These bonds are traded every day, just like any other bond or stock. It's the price and yield of that particular bond that affect interest rates. That's why rates can change throughout the day: because the bonds are being bought and sold by various individuals and institutions.

Mortgage bonds work like any other bond or Treasury note. As the price of a bond goes up, the yield, or interest rate, goes down. Conversely, if the price of a bond goes down, the yield (rate) goes up. As new bonds are introduced for sale, they begin at a *par* price. This price equals 100.00 and will yield whatever the bond issuer thinks it can get, say 5.00 percent.

If the price goes up to 101.00, then the rate goes down. If the price goes to 99.00, then the rate goes up. Each morning, as lenders begin to set their interest rates for the day, they look specifically at the appropriate bond, check its opening price on the markets, and set their rates accordingly.

What makes a bond go up or down? Who moves the price one way or the other? The markets determine the price in open trading. And that price is motivated by economic events; the prospect of inflation or even a political event can cause a bond to move one way or the other.

An increase in demand for a stock or mutual fund allows the seller to raise the price. It is being "bid up" by the market. So if more money is leaving bonds, what is happening to the price of those bonds? Right; it's got to go down to attract buyers. When the price of a bond goes down, the yield (the interest rate) goes up.

Historically, when the economy is going well, interest rates rise. When the economy is headed south, rates fall. At least, that's the overall picture. There can be other factors that determine a mortgage bond's price, such as a major political event or crisis, but the most important is the expectation of a booming economy or the anticipation of a recession.

That's who sets mortgage rates. The markets. Or, more specifically, the credit markets. So why in the world does everyone jump when a Fed official talks? Many people jump because they think that's what they're supposed to do. But what the Federal Reserve Board does, among other things, is to control the cost of money and control inflation.

When the Fed raises or lowers rates, it raises or lowers only one or two rates. Specifically, the Fed raises or lowers either the discount rate or the federal funds rate. The discount rate is the rate at which banks borrow money from the federal government. Banks can use this money to make other loans to consumers or businesses and can use this rate to index future loans.

The federal funds rate, or fed funds, is the rate at which banks can borrow from one another on a very short term basis, such as while you're asleep at night. When banks make loans, be it automobile loans, student loans, or home loans, they have to keep in mind their reserve requirements. The reserve requirement is an amount of cash, stated as a percentage of loans made, that the bank is required by the Fed to keep.

If a bank makes a bunch of loans, it might find itself a little less "liquid" and be forced to borrow from other banks to meet its reserve requirement. Remember that funds deposited with a bank are usually "on demand" deposits, meaning that anytime you want access to your very own verified funds, you can get them. But if the bank has lent out too much money and doesn't have enough to back up those deposits, it is required by law to replenish its reserves to meet the needs of its customers.

The Fed lowers or raises these two rates to stimulate or limit the growth of the economy. How can messing with rates do that?

If the economy is slow or slowing, the Fed might lower the cost of funds to banks and other lending institutions. Cheap money might encourage businesses to borrow in order to build more factories or hire more workers. If the economy is moving along too quickly and the increased demand for goods and services is slowly increasing the prices of those goods and services, the Fed will increase rates to make money more expensive, slowing down expansion.

As bond traders, including those who trade mortgage bonds, watch the actions of the Federal Reserve, they can determine the demand for mortgage bonds. If the Fed indicates a slowing economy, mortgage bonds will increase in price because of greater demand. This means lower rates. If bond traders see a rosy economy ahead, then the price goes down, increasing interest rates. That's why bonds are sometimes called a "flight to safety." They guarantee a return regardless of what the stock market is doing.

So what's all the talk about the "prime" rate? The Federal Reserve has nothing to do with the prime rate—directly, anyway. Technically, the prime rate is the *Wall Street Journal* prime, the rate that banks charge their best customers to make just about any type of loan those customers want. Each bank sets its own prime rate, but these rates are typically in lockstep with Fed actions. If the discount rate is increased by $1/2$ percent, banks will immediately increase their prime rate by the same amount. Prime is typically 2 percent higher than the federal discount rate and 3.00 percent higher than the fed funds number.

There are a few loans that use the prime rate as their index, but most of these are second mortgages or lines of credit.

Fixed-rate mortgages aren't tied to any index other than their respective mortgage bond. They're not tied to the 30-year Treasury bond or the 10-year Treasury, or any other index, for that matter. Adjustable-rate mortgages are generally tied to the same index. The difference between one lender's ARM quote and another's will be caused not by a different index but by a different margin.

Lenders that quote a 1-year Treasury ARM use the 1-year Treasury as their index, then add their margin. Two lenders that quote a 1-year Treasury ARM, sometimes called the 1-year T-bill, will have the very same base rate. If the quotes to you are different, it's because one lender is charging a higher margin than the other one.

CHAPTER 24

Closing Costs

You knew there was a catch, right? Lenders don't want to make money just from the interest rate, they also want to make money anywhere they can get it. This is America, right? One way they can make extra money is by charging additional fees. And it's not just the lender that can get its hands into your pockets; almost everyone else in the home-buying process will want to charge you money as well.

There are so many different people and services in a typical home loan transaction that not only is it difficult to keep track of all of them, it's even harder to track down how much they're charging for their services and who pays for them.

I'll break these charges down into lender and nonlender charges. In almost any real estate transaction, most of these businesses will charge you:

Appraiser	$300–$500 (more if the value is more than a million)
Attorney	$100–$500 (price will vary depending upon section of the country)
Escrow	$150–$300 Escrow can mean different things in different parts of the country. It can be a closing, or it can be taxes and insurance payments to an account.
Title Insurance	$300 and higher. Many states regulate this fee, which can sometimes be as high as 1 percent of the loan amount.

Survey	$300–$500. Again, this can be higher for complicated or bigger properties.
Tax Cert.	$70
Flood Cert.	$20
Credit Report	$20
Intangible Tax	1–3 percent of the loan amount or sales price
Documents	$200
Recording	$100

Closing costs include a broad swash of fees, terms, and customs. Many people in the real estate business who read this list will no doubt see some omissions or errors. And they'll be right. Closing costs will vary from one state to the next, even sometimes from one county or parish to the next. But this will give you some general guidelines.

Now let's look at possible lender fees. Like anyone else, lenders can charge whatever they can get away with legally and in a free market. And here's where it gets tricky, so tricky that the federal government established guidelines several years ago to address closing costs.

Discount Point	1 percent of the loan amount
Origination Fee	1 percent of the loan amount
Processing	$200–$500
Administration	$200–$500
Document Preparation	$200–$500
Funding Fee	$200–$500
Underwriting	$200–$500
Commitment	$200–$500
Anything Else	$200–$500

Lender fees such as "administrative" or "processing" fees certainly sound important and can be viewed as relevant to the loan process. But they're also "junk" fees—fees that are charged on every loan application that have nothing to do with getting a particular interest rate or loan amount.

Lenders aren't immune to charging junk fees. You can find them anywhere there is a seller and a buyer of a product or service. Some are negotiable and some are not, but almost everyone in the real estate services industry has them.

The challenge of comparing one lender to another is compounded when fees are introduced. And what a particular fee is called is absolutely unimportant. What's important is what all the fees add up to. This may sound rudimentary, but lenders use fees every day to help them market their mortgage products.

"I see my competitor at Giant Bank is charging you $400 for an administrative fee!" a lender will say, and then, with a straight face, look right at you and say, "We don't charge $400 for an administrative fee. Our fee is only $200."

You may think that you're beginning to get a grasp on this process when you find out later that while, yes, the administrative fee was in fact $200 lower, the other lender also added a couple of hundred bucks for processing your loan, which Giant Bank didn't.

Are fees negotiable? Of course they are. Just about anything is negotiable. Will the lender or escrow company agree to waive your fees? Maybe, maybe not. But you at least have to ask.

Before you ask, you need to determine what fees are typically paid by whom during a routine real estate purchase in your area. Different parts of the country have different fee schedules for various services and a generally accepted custom as to who pays what. For example, in one part of the country, it's the seller that provides the lender and the new owners with a new title insurance policy. In other parts of the country, the buyers pay for their own lender policy and the seller pays for the rest. In still other areas, title insurance is split equally between the buyer and the seller. And so on. Before you can negotiate anything, you need to first know what is expected of you, the buyer.

After you determine who typically owes what, you then need to go to work to negotiate closing charges. Work on the nonlenders first. Their prices are typically set, with some variance, and their sales reps or assistants won't have the authority to waive or reduce anything, much less negotiate on their company's behalf.

When getting quotes from real estate service providers, you have to ask up front which fees can be reduced. In most cases, you won't be able to get any discount whatsoever from any company that has its rates set by state statute. These are sometimes called *promulgated* fees because the

fees are set by law. Title insurance or government fees may be promulgated.

Other fees that are difficult to get negotiated or waived are those from
companies who are not selected by you. You can choose your lender, your
insurance agent, and sometimes your appraiser if it's on your lender's
approved appraiser list. But it's usually the Realtors who set up everything else, such as your closing, legal, and document charges. If you
don't make the choice of who is performing the service, don't expect any
negotiations on costs.

Don't despair, though, because the one service provider whom you
did indeed choose is your lender. And lenders do in fact have some wiggle room—although they certainly won't tell you that up front.

Most lenders and mortgage brokers have a couple of fees that they
charge, the most common ones being processing and underwriting.
Sometimes there are other ones in addition to those, but there's a difference between a required fee and a waivable fee. A waivable fee is one
that the lender or mortgage broker would like to get in addition to anything else, but that is not a required charge.

A mortgage company may have an administrative fee that must be
quoted to all customers, but the loan officer may have the authority to
waive that fee in a competitive situation. Which, if you think about it, is
almost every situation.

Fees that may be waived by a lender often don't come out of the loan
officer's pockets. Remember that the loan officer gets a percentage of all
income generated from originating a loan. If a loan officer charges you a
$300 commitment fee, then she will usually get a "split" of that $300. If
the loan officer waives that $300 fee, she loses the potential income from
that charge.

However, a lender can also charge required fees. These fees must be
either collected or somehow otherwise compensated for. For instance,
suppose a loan officer quotes a $300 processing fee and a $250 document preparation fee. He can waive the $300 processing charge without
penalty. He just doesn't make as much money on the loan.

But the $250 may be a required fee. The lender demands it. If in a
competitive situation a loan officer decides to waive not only the $300 proc-

essing charge, but also the $250 document preparation fee, the $250 will be deducted from the loan officer's commission check. A lender will say, "Sure, you can waive that fee to the consumer, but you can't waive it to us."

This practice is quite common. During a hypercompetitive rate quote, when a loan officer is doing everything he can to get the loan, he'll put his own money on the table. When you're negotiating closing fees trying to get the best deal, this is the stage you want to get to. When you start pulling money from the loan officer's pocketbook, the real negotiations begin. You don't think this happens? I've seen it happen nearly every day.

Still another way to have your closing fees reduced, or even paid for altogether, is to have the lender pay for them. That's right, the lender. Sure, the loan officer can waive a fee or two, but there is a way to get a lender to pay those fees. Sometimes all of them.

Lenders can do this by adjusting your interest rate. Almost every lender will offer to pay your closing fees if you choose a higher interest rate. Oh, yeah, some deal. Actually, it is a good deal. Just as a consumer can pay 1 point to buy her rate down by $1/4$ percent, she can do the reverse and increase her rate by $1/4$ percent, and the lender then pays the consumer 1 point.

No, the lender can't give you cash at closing, but because you chose a slightly higher interest rate, the lender has some credit that it can direct toward your fees. Let's look at an example.

Suppose the loan amount is $500,000 and the rate is 6.50 percent on a 30-year fixed-rate note. Your monthly payment is $3,160, and your closing costs add up to $6,000. If you increase your interest rate by $1/4$ percent, your monthly payment goes to $3,242, or an increase of $82. In this scenario, you increased your payment by $82, or $1/4$ percent, and had the lender credit you 1 discount point, or $5,000.

Your lender can now pay $5,000 of your closing costs, leaving only $1,000 for you to pay. Okay, okay, I know. If you increase your rate by $1/4$ percent, then it's not the lender who in fact pays your fees—it's you in the form of a higher rate. And that's correct. But if you divide that $82 into the $5,000 credit you earned, you'll find that it will be more than five years before that higher rate gets the upper hand. You can invest that money and make more with it in five years.

Buying a house, especially when money for a down payment and closing costs is precious, can be expensive. But by adjusting your rate to pay for those costs, you can sometimes gain some leverage. And every lender can make that offer.

Still there's another way to have your closing costs reduced: Have the seller pay for them.

Easier said than done? Maybe, but why not ask? Everything is negotiable, right? But you'll never know until you make your offer. Your Realtor can help you structure your offer to give you the greatest chance for a successful negotiation, and sellers make concessions every single day.

If the seller says no to your request that she pay your closing costs, then regroup and counter with another offer that will satisfy everyone's demands. Say that a house is for sale at $300,000. You offer $290,000 with the seller paying $5,000 of your closing costs. If the seller says yes, then you win. If not, change your tactic.

This time, increase your offer by $5,000, the amount of your closing fees, and again ask the seller to pay $5,000 toward your closing costs. This time you both win. The seller gets what she wanted with regard to the selling price of the home and still netted the same amount, despite paying your closing costs.

Okay, sure. You've increased your loan amount by $5,000 but the difference is marginal when you leveraged that $5,000. At 6.50 percent on a 30-year fixed-rate note for $290,000, your payment is $1,832 per month. When you increase your loan amount to $295,000, your payment goes only to $1,864, an increase of just $32. And you don't have to pay $5,000 in out-of-pocket closing fees.

Closing costs on any loan can't just vanish. Someone will have to pay for them. But with a little creativity and the right loan officer, you can make sure that you're not the one that has to write the check for them.

Federal Regulations and Closing Costs

Fortunately, there are some regulations that apply to mortgage loans and fees. Unfortunately, these come from the government. That tells you a

lot right there—there is an attempt to protect consumers from unscrupu-
lous lenders, but often the laws, the interpretation of those laws, and the
enforcement of those laws leaves a lot to be desired. But hey, they're
trying.

Lenders are required to disclose to you their closing fees, and everyone else's for that matter, at the time of the loan application if you met
face to face. If you completed an online application or mailed or faxed
your application, the lender is supposed to disclose those fees to you
within three business days of receipt of your application. This is a federal
law. The estimate is officially called the Good Faith Estimate of Closing
Costs, or simply the GFE.

The GFE will be accompanied by another legal form called the Truth
in Lending Disclosure, or TIL. Both of these forms attempt to explain to
you not only what fees you're likely to encounter when you show up for
your closing, but also things such as the amount of interest paid over the
life of the loan, your note rate, your APR, and your finance charges.

The GFE is fairly straightforward, but the TIL is anything but.

The GFE is divided into six distinct sections beginning with section
800 (I'm not kidding), 900, 1000, and then of course 1100. Followed by
1200 and 1300. Each line item within that series will apply to a particular
fee.

Section 800 is reserved for the lender and its service partners. Those
service partners include credit report companies, appraisers, issuers of
flood certificates, and tax service companies. Any charge from any of
those firms will appear in this section. Line item 801, for example, is
reserved for a lender's origination fee, while line 803 is for the appraisal.
Don't be scared; there aren't 100 line items in Section 800, and you
probably won't see more than seven or eight entries. Section 800 is
where you'll find all the lender "junk" fees.

Section 1100 is reserved for all title and settlement charges, including escrow fees, attorneys' charges, and fees for closing. Anything that is
generated by or on the behalf of the title company will show up here.

Section 1200 contains fees associated with the government. Recording fees, tax stamps, and similar charges will be listed here.

Section 1300 is for just about anything else. You'll find pest inspection charges, survey and abstract fees, and anything else that doesn't have some other place.

Section 900 is for anything that needs to be paid up front or in advance. These are often called "prepaid" items and include homeowner's insurance premiums and any taxes that are due.

Finally, in Section 1000, you'll see line items for funds collected to establish insurance, tax, and homeowners' association impound or escrow accounts.

You must sign the GFE and return it to the lender. You keep a copy for yourself, but the lender will have to verify that it in fact sent you the GFE within three days or provided it to you at the time of your loan application. If the lender ever got audited by HUD, for example, and couldn't prove that it provided you with the GFE within the accepted period, this could be written up as a violation. Enough of those violations and the lender can be fined and, worse, made ineligible to originate government loans.

The Truth in Lending Disclosure will attempt to explain certain characteristics of your loan. First, it will tell you how much you're borrowing and at what rate. If the rate is fixed, you'll see that, and if it's an ARM, you'll see that too, along with the potential adjustment periods.

There's a special section labeled "Finance Charges" that is reserved for lender fees. It's these fees that are used to calculate the APR. Next to that number, you'll see your amount financed. This number might surprise you, as it's the principal balance less the finance charges. This is the number used to calculate the APR. The algorithm for APR first calculates the monthly payment based upon the terms of your note, then recalculates the interest rate having subtracting the finance charges from your original loan amount.

Unless you're a mathematician, you're going to have to trust me on that one, but that's how the APR is calculated.

"Amount Borrowed" is your principal balance plus all interest accrued if you took your loan to full term. That's a big number, and, no, you're not obligated to pay that number if you sell the home early or refinance.

The TIL will also explain when your payment would be considered late, if there are any prepayment penalties on the loan, and whether you're entitled to be refunded any finance charges should you pay the loan off early.

The GFE and TIL can help consumers better understand the financial aspects of buying a house, but quite frankly there are loan officers who simply gloss over the TIL and who can't explain the APR number, much less the amount financed. If you have questions about the TIL, ask the loan officer. If he can't help, ask his boss. It's better to understand what's going on than not, right? And in these days of computers, these forms are spit out on a daily basis with the loan officer not really knowing how or why they're calculated.

The Good Faith Estimate is easier to understand. It shows who's charging you for what. The amount isn't supposed to vary when you show up for closing, but it invariably does. In fact, consumers have been screwed so many times at the closing table with a few hundred dollars here and a few hundred dollars there that the government set up all these new rules to protect us.

The problem is, what's a borrower to do when she's trying to close on her new house and the settlement statement is off by about $500 in fees from the lender that weren't originally disclosed? Cancel the closing? Lose the house?

There's not much wiggle room. At least, there used not to be. Now consumers can take those settlement papers in hand and get their money back. There is a generally accepted rule of thumb that if the APR at closing varies by more than 1/8 percent from what was originally disclosed, then the lender is in violation. If a consumer signs a GFE with an APR of 5.78 percent and the final settlement shows additional charges resulting in an APR of 6.25 percent, that lender is in violation. But there's no exact litmus test; the 1/8 percent variance is just a guideline.

The problem is that the government has a lot on its plate. There's not much you can do individually. If you feel you've been had, then contact HUD at:

U.S. Department of HUD
Office of RESPA and Interstate Land Sales

451 7th Street, SW, Room 9154
Washington, DC 20410

The big surprises at closing are usually a result of nonlender charges. Every lender knows its own charges. There's no guesswork. Sometimes, though, another party is added to the transaction that the lender may not be familiar with. Remember, it's the lender that has to provide the GFE. If a lender doesn't know what a particular attorney or insurance agent is going to charge you at closing, it has to guess. They do so in "good faith."

Closing cost disclosure issues fall under the umbrella of the oft-addressed Real Estate Settlement Procedures Act of 1974, or RESPA as it's commonly known.

RESPA's purpose is to help consumers shop for loans and to (hopefully) eliminate kickbacks and referral fees. The consumer typically uses whomever the Realtor refers him to, and simply has to use whomever the Realtor chooses for title, legal, and closing. The consumer has a right to know if the Realtor is getting any money for a referral fee and has a right to know exactly how much something costs.

Kickbacks aren't allowed. A Realtor or any other service provider is prohibited from accepting money or anything else of value for referring business to someone else. If Joe Attorney gives Sally Realtor $100 for every referral, that's against the law.

If, however, there is a legal arrangement between Joe and Sally, and the fee is disclosed to you both up front and at closing, then that $100 is perfectly okay. If a Realtor gets a 6 percent commission at closing, you'll see that on your final settlement statement. If the insurance agent is charging you $1,000 for insurance, you'll see that as well. In fact, all charges and fees that absolutely anyone is getting that are related to your home purchase are supposed to be listed here. If they aren't, it's against the law.

Consumers also have the right to know if a lender pays $15 for a credit report but charges you $20 for that same report. Or maybe an appraisal costs $300, but the lender charges you $325. These "up charges" aren't legal, at least as of this writing. But even if they were legal, you have a right to know about them, according to RESPA.

Appendix A: The 10 Biggest Mistakes Mortgage Applicants Make

1. Prejudging their situation and never applying for a loan.
2. Assuming that their credit won't let them qualify.
3. Misqualifying themselves because of outdated debt ratio guidelines.
4. Applying directly with a subprime lender without trying conventional first.
5. Failing to shop their mortgage around to other lenders.
6. Not asking questions when they're unclear about something.
7. Comparing different loan types with one another.
8. Paying too much in closing costs and points.
9. Being embarrassed about their credit situation.
10. Falling victim to predatory lending.

Appendix B: Additional Resources

www.realtor.com   The official web site for the National Association of Realtors. This is a good place to start looking for a home if you have no idea where to start. You can type in your desired location, how much you want to pay, and so on. You can also find a list of Realtors if you don't have one yet. You can find a lender or a mover, and you can pick up some handy consumer information about home buying.

www.hud.gov   A big site, owned and paid for with taxpayer dollars, that gives you everything you need to know about FHA loans, buying, selling, owning, renting—you name it. It's very consumer friendly and a nice starting place if you're thinking of getting an FHA mortgage loan.

www.fanniemae.com   The web site of the Federal National Mortgage Association, or Fannie Mae. It's a huge site, with lots of consumer information as well as data on new mortgage projects by Fannie Mae.

www.freddiemac.com   The web site of the Federal Home Loan Mortgage Corporation, or Freddie Mac. It provides standard fare, with lots of information for consumers—a great web site for gobs of loan information.

www.homebuilder.com   The official web site for the National Association of Homebuilders. It's very much like the site at www.realtor.com, but it lists only new homes or homes that are under construction. You can view new homes by location and price range as well as look at new home plans online. Need some names of builders? You can find that list here as well.

www.va.gov   The web site for VA loans. It provides information on VA loans and how to qualify for them, along with forms that qualified veterans might need. This section is actually a subset of the Department of Veterans Affairs site, but it has a direct link from the main page to the home loan section.

www.fsbo.com   A web site listing For Sale by Owner, or FSBO (pronounced fizz-bow), homes from all parts of the country. Some homes never make it to a multiple listing service, and for those that don't, there's a place where people want to save some real estate commission and sell the home themselves.

www.usda.gov   The home for all information about rural home loans from the federal government. It explains in detail all the information about qualifying for USDA loans, where they're available, and who qualifies.

www.myfico.com   A site owned by Fair Isaac Corporation, the company that developed the FICO score, which has information on credit, credit scores, and credit reports. Even though consumers are allowed to get one free credit report per year, there may be times when you need another.

www.bbb.com   The site for the Better Business Bureau. Here you can type in a company's business name, its web address, or its telephone number, and the Better Business Bureau will check its records to see if it has any information or complaint about that company.

www.realtytimes.com   A great site for both Realtors and consumers. Award-winning real estate and finance columnists post articles on this free site.

www.nehemiah.com   One of the most popular sites that explains how down payment assistance programs work and gives a list of lenders who participate in the program. It's geared toward new houses but is also a resource for existing homes as well.

www.annualcreditreport.com   The official web site where you can get your free annual credit report as required by the FACTA Act of 2003.

Appendix C:
HUD-Approved Nonprofit Agencies and Home Buyer Assistance Resources

Philadelphia Region as Reported by the Department of Housing and Urban Development

Asian Americans for Equality, Inc.	Planning & Development	New York	NY
Columbus Housing Partnership	562 East Main Street	Columbus	OH
Economic Opportunity Council of Suffolk County	475 East Main Street, Suite 206	Patchogue	NY
Greater Baltimore OIC (Opportunities, Inc.)	1521 Homestead Street	Baltimore	MD
Home Headquarters Inc.	120 East Jefferson Street	Syracuse	NY
Housing Initiative Partnership, Inc.	4310 Gallatin Street, 3rd Floor	Hyattsville	MD
Housing Resources of Columbia County, Inc.	605 State Street	Hudson	NY
Neighborhood Housing Services—New Britain	223 Broad Street	New Britain	CT
New Life Development, Inc.	2811 Granby Street	Norfolk	VA
NHS Community Development Corporation	121 West 27th Street	New York	NY
Northfield Community Local Development Corp.	160 Heberton Avenue	Staten Island	NY
Snyderville Community Development Center	2013 South Seventh Street	Philadelphia	PA

Virginia Beach Community Development Corporation	2700 International Parkway, Suite 300	Virginia Beach	VA
Virginia Supportive Housing	5 South Adams St. (P.O. Box 12123)	Richmond	VA
Adopt a House	100 Prospect Street, Suite S-201	Stamford	CT
Better Neighborhoods, Inc.	986 Albany Street	Schenectady	NY
Blue Ridge Housing Development Corporation	P.O. Box 11683, 510 11th Street, NW	Roanoke	VA
Center for Community Development	440 High Street, Suite 204	Portsmouth	VA
Columbus Housing Partnership	562 East Main Street	Columbus	OH
Community Renewal Team of Greater Hartford	555 Windsor Street	Hartford	CT
Co-op Initiatives, Inc.	20-28 Sargeant Street, Suite 102	Hartford	CT
District of Columbia Housing Finance Agency	815 Florida Avenue, NW	Washington	DC
Eastern Connecticut Housing Opportunities (ECHO)	105 Huntington Street	New London	CT
First Ward Action Council, Inc.	167 Clinton Street	Binghamton	NY
Friends of the Homeless (2 of 2)	1600-25th Street	Newport News	VA
Greater Niles Community Development Corporation	210 East Main Street, P.O. Box 11	Niles	MI
Greater Washington Urban League, Inc.	3501 14th Street, NW	Washington	DC
HAP, Inc.—Hampden Hampshire Housing Partnership	322 Main Street	Springfield	MA
Home Partnership, Inc.	Rumsey Tower Building	Joppatowne	MD
Jackson Affordable Housing Corporation	161 West Michigan Avenue	Jackson	MI
Jewish Vocational Service	29699 Southfield Road	Southfield	MI

Atlanta Region as Reported by the Department of Housing and Urban Development

Cape Coral Housing Development Corp.	1430-B.S.E. 16th Place	Cape Coral	FL
Central Florida Community Development Corp.	P.O. Box 15065	Daytona Beach	FL

Clearwater Neighborhood Housing Services, Inc.	608 North Garden Avenue	Clearwater	FL
Community Service Foundation, Inc.	925 Lakeview Road	Clearwater	FL
Ecumenical Developments, Inc.	2038 NW 5th Place	Miami	FL
Friends of Lubavitch of Florida	1140 Alton Road	Miami Beach	FL
Haven Economic Development, Inc.	8612 S.R. 84	Davie	FL
L.E.S., Inc.—Liberia Economic & Social Development, Inc.	2207 Raleigh Street	Hollywood	FL
Neighborhood Housing & Development Corp.	633 N.W. 8th Avenue	Gainesville	FL
South Florida Affordable Housing Corp.	12865 W. Dixie Highway	North Miami Beach	FL
United Development Communities Inc.	3706 North Ocean Blvd., #370	Fort Lauderdale	FL
Affordable Housing Assistance	1470 Maria Lane, Suite 380	Walnut Creek	CA
Amerihome, Inc.	P.O. Box 50126	Atlanta	GA
Antioch Ministries	1451 Florence Street/ P.O. Box 6	Augusta	GA
Cobb Housing, Inc.	268 Lawrence Street, Suite A	Marietta	GA
Columbus Housing Initiative, Inc.	18 11th Street, Suite A	Columbus	GA
East Athens Development Corp	410 McKinley Drive	Athens	GA
Family Housing Revitalization Program, Inc.	3355 Lenox Road, Suite 750	Atlanta	GA
Gainesville–Hall County Neighborhood Revitalization	430 Prior Street, P.O. Box 642	Gainesville	GA
Housecalls International—Atlanta	P.O. Box 82741	Conyers	GA
Housing and Economic Leadership Partners Inc.	485 Huntington Rd, Suite 200	Athens	GA
Mission Outreach Centers, Inc.	2115 South Madison Street	Albany	GA
Promise Land Community Development	313 D Telfair Street	Augusta	GA

Reynoldstown Revitalization Corporation	100 Flat Shoals Avenue, P.O. Box 89092	Atlanta	GA
Southeast Georgia Community Development Corp	1416 Albany Street	Brunswick	GA
United Way of Metropolitan Atlanta	100 Edgewood Avenue, NE	Atlanta	GA
ACORN Housing Corporation of Illinois	650 S. Clark St. Ste 301	Chicago	IL
Bethel Human Resources, Inc.	14931 South Lincoln Avenue	Harvey	IL
Bethel New Life, Inc.	4950 West Thomas Street	Chicago	IL
CEDA Neighborhood Development Corporation	208 South LaSalle Street, Suite 1900	Chicago	IL
Christian Home Network	744 Suncrest Drive	Aurora	IL
Cook County Housing Dev. Corp	310 South Michigan	Chicago	IL

Denver Region as Reported by the Department of Housing and Urban Development

Telephone Number	Name of Organization	City	State	Type of Agency	Comments	Approved Areas of Operation
APPROVED APPLICATIONS (Sorted Alphabetical by STATE, then by NAME OF ORGANIZATION)						
870-935-8610	Crowley's Ridge Development Council	Jonesboro	AR	Nonprofit corporation	REO sales	Craighead, Greene, Jackson, Poinsette, Cross, Crittenden, St, Francis, and Woodruff Counties
501-478-9141	Lend A Hand, Inc.	Barling	AR	Nonprofit corporation	Secondary financing	Arkansas Counties of Crawford and Sebastian
415-616-2680	Federal Home Loan Bank of San Francisco	San Francisco	CA	Government sponsored	Down payment assistance grants	
303-428-1448	Colorado Rural Housing Development	Westminster	CO	Nonprofit corporation	REO sales, FHA financing, secondary financing	Colorado Counties of Adams, Broomfield, Denver, Jefferson, El Paso, and Teller
303-477-4774	Del Norte Neighborhood Development Corp.	Denver	CO	Nonprofit corporation	REO sales, FHA financing, secondary financing	Within a 200-mile radius of Denver MSA
303-860-7747	Hope Communities, Inc.	Denver	CO	Nonprofit corporation	REO sales, secondary financing	City and County of Denver

Telephone Number	Name of Organization	City	State	Type of Agency	Comments	Approved Areas of Operation
970-259-1086	Housing Solutions for the Southwest	Durango	CO	Nonprofit corporation	REO sales, secondary financing	Colorado Counties of Archuleta, Dolores, La Plata, Montezuma, and San Juan
303-830-3300	Mercy Housing Southwest	Denver	CO	Nonprofit corporation	REO sales—limited to 12 properties at one time	Within a 200-mile radius of Denver, Co
719-544-8078	Neighborhood Housing Services of Pueblo, Inc	Pueblo	CO	Nonprofit corporation	Secondary financing	City of Pueblo, CO
720-946-9022	Neighborhood Partners	Denver	CO	Nonprofit corporation	REO sales	Denver MSA, CO
303-534-8342	NEWSED Community Development Corporation	Denver	CO	Nonprofit corporation	REO sales, secondary financing	City and County of Denver, CO
970-542-0955	Northeast Colorado Housing, Inc.	Fort Morgan	CO	Nonprofit corporation	Secondary financing. CHDO— Counties of Logan, Morgan, Phillips, Sedgewick, Washington, and Yuma	Logan, Morgan, Phillips, Sedgwick, Yuma, and Washington Counties, Colorado
303-934-8057	Southwest Improvement Council dba Southwest Neighborhood Housing	Denver	CO	Nonprofit corporation	REO sales, secondary financing	City and County of Denver, CO
303-275-3452	STRIDE	Lakewood	CO	Nonprofit corporation	Secondary financing	Colorado Counties of Adams, Arapahoe, Broomfield, Denver, Douglas, and Jefferson
303-894-9689	Women of the Word Ministries Int'l	Denver	CO	Nonprofit corporation	REO sales, FHA financing	Colorado Counties of Adams, Arapahoe, Boulder, Denver, Douglas, El Paso, Jefferson, Summit. Weld, Huerfano, Archuleta, Conejos, Montezuma, and Alamosa

Telephone Number	Name of Organization	City	State	Type of Agency	Comments	Approved Areas of Operation
712-328-6602	Community Housing Investment Corp.	Council Bluffs	IA	Nonprofit corporation	Secondary financing—this approval applies only to the City of Council Bluffs down payment program	The City of Council Bluffs, IA
800-544-3452	Federal Home Loan Bank of Des Moines	Des Moines	IA	Government sponsored	Down payment assistance grants	
312-565-5725	Federal Home Loan Bank of Chicago	Chicago	IL	Government sponsored	Down payment assistance grants	
785-233-0507	Federal Home Loan Bank of Topeka	Topeka	KS	Government sponsored	Down payment assistance grants	
504-899-5900	Neighborhood Housing Services of New Orleans, Inc.	New Orleans	LA	Nonprofit corporation	Secondary financing	New Orleans, LA metropolitan area
763-783-4747	Anoka County Community Action Program	Blaine	MN	Nonprofit corporation	Secondary financing	Anoka County, MN
320-259-0393	Central Minnesota Housing Partnership	St. Cloud	MN	Nonprofit Corporation	Secondary financing	Minnesota Counties of Aitkin, Benton, Carlton, Cass, Chisago, Crow Wing, Isanti, Kanabee, Mille Lacs, Morrison, Pine, Sherburne, Stearns, Todd, Wadena, and Wright
507-287-7117	First Homes Properties	Rochester	MN	Nonprofit corporation	REO sales	Minnesota Counties of Olmsted, Goddhue, Dodge, Mower, Fillmore, Winona, and Wabasha
651-221-1997	Greater Minnesota Housing Fund	St. Paul	MN	Nonprofit corporation	Rochester (MN) First Homes Program—secondary financing and Gap Loan Program—secondary financing	Minnesota counties within a 200-mile radius of St. Paul, MN

Telephone Number	Name of Organization	City	State	Type of Agency	Comments	Approved Areas of Operation
218-444-4732	Headwaters Housing Development Corp	Bemidji	MN	Nonprofit corporation	Secondary financing	Minnesota Counties of Beltrami, Clearwater, Hubbard, Lake of the Woods, and Mahnomen
218-327-6711	KOOTASCA Community Action	Grand Rapids	MN	Nonprofit corporation	Secondary financing	Minnesota Counties of Isasca and Koochinching
218-727-8604	Neighborhood Housing Services of Duluth	Duluth	MN	Nonprofit corporation	Secondary financing	Approved for the following areas: Duluth metropolitan area
612-724-1502	Powderhorn Community Council	Minneapolis	MN	Nonprofit corporation	Secondary financing	Minneapolis, MN metropolitan area
507-282-0203	Rochester Area Foundation	Rochester	MN	Nonprofit corporation	Rochester (MN) First Homes Program— secondary financing	Rochester, MN metropolitan area
612-673-0477	West Bank Community Housing Corp	Minneapolis	MN	Nonprofit corporation	Secondary financing	Minneapolis–St. Paul metropolitan area
314-367-3440	Better Family Life, Inc.	St. Louis	MO	Nonprofit corporation	Secondary financing	St. Louis, MO metropolitan area
314-862-8130	Beyond Housing / Neighborhood Housing Services	St. Louis	MO	Nonprofit corporation	Secondary financing	The City and County of St. Louis, MO
402-379-3311	Elkhorn Valley CDC	Norfolk	NE	Nonprofit corporation	REO sales, secondary financing	Nebraska Counties of Madison, Stanton, Cuming, Wayne, Pierce, Antelope, Platte, and Colfax
402-435-0315	Nebraska Housing Development Assn	Lincoln	NE	Nonprofit corporation	Secondary financing	The portion of the State of Nebraska located within a 200-mile radius of Lincoln, NE
505-989-3960	Santa Fe Community Housing Trust	Santa Fe	NM	Nonprofit corporation	Secondary financing	City and County of Santa Fe, NM
701-636-5860	Eastern Dakota Housing Alliance	Hillsboro	ND	Nonprofit corporation	Secondary financing	North Dakota Counties of Barnes, Benson, Cass, Cavalier, Dickey, Eddy, Foster, Grand Forks, Griggs, Kidder, La Moure, Logan,

Telephone Number	Name of Organization	City	State	Type of Agency	Comments	Approved Areas of Operation
						McIntosh, Nelson, Pembina, Ramsey, Ransom, Richland, Rolette, Sargent, Steele, Stutsman, Towner, Traill, Walsh, and Wells
701-255-4591	Lewis & Clark Community Works	Bismarck	ND	Nonprofit corporation	Secondary financing	
405-232-0199	Community Action Agency of Oklahoma City/ Oklahoma and Canadian Counties	Oklahoma City	OK	Nonprofit corporation	Secondary financing	City of Oklahoma, Oklahoma Counties of Oklahoma and Canadian, excluding Midwest City
918-382-3240	Community Action Project of Tulsa County	Tulsa	OK	Instrumentality of government	REO sales, FHA financing, secondary financing	
918-341-5000	Community Action Resource & Development	Claremore	OK	Nonprofit corporation	Secondary financing	Oklahoma Counties of Mayes, Nowata, Rogers, Wagoner, and Washington
605-578-1401	Neighborhood Housing Services of the Black Hills, Inc.	Deadwood	SD	Nonprofit corporation	REO sales, secondary financing	City of Wall, MT, Counties of Lawrence, Meade, and Butte, MT
605-394-4181	Rapid City Community Development Corp.	Rapid City	SD	Nonprofit corporation	Secondary financing	Pennington County, SD
605-339-0942	Sioux Empire Housing Partnership	Sioux Falls	SD	Nonprofit corporation	REO sales	South Dakota Counties of Minnehalia, Lincoln, Turner, and McCook
956-541-4955	Community Development Corp. of Brownsville	Brownsville	TX	Nonprofit corporation	Secondary financing	County of Cameron, TX
940-484-7048	Denton Affordable Housing Corporation	Denton	TX	Nonprofit corporation	REO sales, FHA financing, secondary financing	Denton County, TX
214-651-7789	EHOP-Dallas, Inc.	Dallas	TX	Nonprofit corporation	REO sales	Dallas County, TX
214-651-7789	The Enterprise Foundation	Dallas	TX	Nonprofit corporation	Secondary financing—	City of Dallas, TX

Telephone Number	Name of Organization	City	State	Type of Agency	Comments	Approved Areas of Operation
					administering funds for City of Dallas's MAP	
800-362-2944	Federal Home Loan Bank of Dallas	Dallas	TX	Government sponsored	Down payment assistance grants	
972-253-8336	Irving Community Development Corp.	Irving	TX	Nonprofit corporation	Secondary financing	The City of Irving, TX
409-880-3763	Jefferson County Housing Finance Corp	Beaumont	TX	Instrumentality of government	REO sales, FHA financing, secondary financing	
956-712-9100	Laredo-Webb NHS	Laredo	TX	Nonprofit corporation	Secondary financing	City of Laredo, Webb County, and counties contiguous to Webb County, TX
254-752-1647	Neighborhood Housing Services of Waco	Waco	TX	Nonprofit corporation	Secondary financing	City of Waco, TX and surrounding areas within a 200-mile radius
210-433-2787	Our Casas Resident Council	San Antonio	TX	Nonprofit corporation	Secondary financing	Bexar County, TX
214-824-7555	Restoration Community	Dallas	TX	Nonprofit corporation	REO sales	Texas Counties of Dallas, Rockwall, Kaufman, and Collin
281-484-4663	South Plains Community Action Assoc.	Levelland	TX	Nonprofit corporation	Secondary financing	Texas Counties of Bailey, Cochran, Garza, Hockley, Lamb, Lynn, Terry, and Yoakum
817-924-5091	Tarrant County Housing Partnership, Inc.	Fort Worth	TX	Nonprofit corporation	REO sales, secondary financing	Tarrant County, TX
801-994-7222	Community Development Corporation of Utah	Salt Lake City	UT	Nonprofit corporation	ACA participant, REO sales, secondary financing	Properties within a 200-mile radius of Salt Lake City, UT
801-375-5820	Neighborhood Housing Services of Provo	Provo	UT	Nonprofit corporation	Secondary financing	Provo, UT
920-448-3075	Neighborhood Housing Services of Green Bay	Green Bay	WI	Nonprofit corporation	REO sales, secondary financing	Brown County, WI

Telephone Number	Name of Organization	City	State	Type of Agency	Comments	Approved Areas of Operation
414-449-9914	Neighborhood Housing Services of Milwaukee	Milwaukee	WI	Nonprofit corporation	Secondary financing	Milwaukee, WI metropolitan area
414-562-5070	Select Milwaukee	Milwaukee	WI	Nonprofit corporation	Rehabilitation assistance, secondary financing limited to the following employee homeownership programs: Alexian Village, Aurora, Covenant Health Care, Harley-Davidson Motor Co., Milwaukee Public Schools, Milwaukee Rescue Mission, Milwaukee Women's Center, MGIC, Northwestern Mutual, YWCA, Visa Lighting Corp., Wisconsin Humane Society	Milwaukee, WI metropolitan area
206-340-2300	Federal Home Loan Bank of Seattle	Seattle	WA	Government sponsored	Down payment assistance grants	

West Region as Provided by the Department of Housing and Urban Development

Affordable Housing Assistance	1470 Maria Lane, #380	Walnut Creek	CA	94596	(925) 932-8200
Anchorage Neighborhood Housing Services	480 West Tudor Road	Anchorage	AK	99503	(714) 372-2223
AOF/Pacific Affordable Housing	7777 Center Ave., #240	Huntington Beach	CA	92647	(714) 799-1339
Blue Mountain Action Council	342 Catherine Street	Walla Walla	CA	99362	(509) 529-4980

Bothhands	P.O. Box 30134	Flagstaff	AZ	86003	(928) 214-7456
Campesinos Unidos, Inc.	1005 "C" Street	Brawley	CA	92227	(760) 344-4500
Century Center for Economic Opportunity	17216 South Figueroa Street	Gardena	CA	90248	(310) 225-3060
Community Development Agency Inc.	13754 Loumont Street	Whittier	CA	90601	(562) 760-1213
Community Housing Dev. of North Richmond	1535A 3rd Street	Richmond	CA	94801	(510) 412-9290
East Las Vegas CDC	3031 East Charleston Blvd., #C	Las Vegas	NV	89101	(702) 307-1710
Enterprise Home Ownership Partners, Inc.	315 West 9th Street, #801	Los Angeles	CA	90015	(213) 833-0053
Esperanza Community Housing Corp.	2337 South Figueroa Street	Los Angeles	CA	90007	(213) 748-7285
Foundation for Social Resource	4029 Westerly Place, #101	Newport Beach	CA	92660	(949) 253-3120
Fresno West Coalition for Economic Development	302 Fresno Street, #212 & 213	Fresno	CA	93706	(559) 263-1000
Hart Community Homes	2807 East Lincoln Avenue	Anaheim	CA	92806	(714) 630-1007
Hometown Community Development Corp	320 Pine Avenue, #905	Long Beach	CA	90802	(562) 301-7313
(H.O.M.S.) Housing Opportunities Management Services	2417 Bank Drive, Suite B-2	Boise	ID	83705	(208) 389-9231
Housing Action Resource Trust (HART)	8711 Monroe Court, Suite A	Rancho Cucamonga	CA	91730	(909) 945-1574
Inland Valley EDC	363 South Park Avenue, #104	Pomona	CA	91766	(909) 623-1946
Kern County Economic Opportunity Corp.	300 19th Street	Bakersfield	CA	93301	(661) 336-5236
Mary Erickson Community Housing Corp.	300 South El Camino Real, #211	San Clemente	CA	92672	(949) 369-5419

My Friends House Assembly	6525 South Norwalk Blvd.	Whittier	CA	90606	(562) 692-0953
Neighborhood Housing Service of Boise	P.O. Box 8223	Boise	ID	83707	(208) 343-4065
Neighborhood Housing Service of Phoenix	320 East McDowell, #120	Phoenix	AZ	85004	(602) 258-1659
Neighborhood Housing Services of the Inland Empire	1390 North "D" Street	San Bernardino	CA	92405	(909) 884-6891
New Image Emergency Shelter for the Homeless	401 East Ocean Blvd., #206	Long Beach	CA	90802	(562) 983-7289
NHS Neighborhood Redevelopment Corp.	3926 Wilshire Blvd., #200	Los Angeles	CA	90010	(213) 381-2862
Pacific Community Services, Inc.	329 Railroad Avenue	Pittsburg	CA	94565	(925) 439-1056
Phoenix Programs	1875 Willow Pass Road, #300	Concord	CA	94520	(925) 825-4700
Pocatello Neighborhood Housing Services	206 North Arthur	Pocatello	ID	83204	(208) 232-9468
Primavera Builders Inc.	151 West 40th Street	South Tucson	AZ	85713	(520) 882-5383
Riverside Housing Dev.	4250 Brockton Ave., #200	Riverside	CA	92501	(909) 341-6511
Rose Community Development	5215 SE Duke Street	Portland	OR	97206	(503) 788-8052
Shepherd of the Hills	30121 Niguel Road	Laguna	CA	92677	(949) 495-1310
Stocktonians Taking Action (STAND)	P.O. Box 30231	Stockton	CA	95213	(209) 937-7625
Tentmakers Missionary Fellowship	125 North Lincoln Street, #E	Dixon	CA	95620	(707) 693-8368
United Care, Inc.	3699 Crenshaw Blvd.	Los Angeles	CA	90016	(323) 508-0200
Women's Development Center	953 East Sahara Avenue, #201	Las Vegas	NV	89104	(702) 796-7770
Anchorage Neighborhood Housing Services	480 West Tudor Road	Anchorage	AK	99503	(714) 372-2223
Bothhands	P.O. Box 30134	Flagstaff	AZ	86003	(928) 214-7456
Neighborhood Housing Service of Boise	P.O. Box 8223	Boise	ID	83707	(208) 343-4065

Neighborhood Housing Service of Phoenix	320 East McDowell, #120	Phoenix	AZ	85004	(602) 258-1659
Pocatello Neighborhood Housing Services	206 North Arthur	Pocatello	ID	83204	(208) 232-9468
Riverside Housing Dev.	4250 Brockton Ave., #200	Riverside	CA	92501	(909) 341-6511
Women's Development Center	953 East Sahara Avenue, #201	Las Vegas	NV	89104	(702) 796-7770

Appendix D:
Payment Tables

Payments per Thousand Dollars Financed

Find the interest rate, move across to the Term column, and multiply that number by the number of thousand dollars financed.

Example: 6.50 percent, 30-year term on $150,000

$6.32 × 150 (thousands) = $948.00 principal and interest payment

Rate	40 years	30 years	25 years	20 years	15 years	10 years
2.500	$3.30	$3.95	$4.49	$5.30	$6.67	$9.43
2.625	$3.37	$4.02	$4.55	$5.36	$6.73	$9.48
2.750	$3.44	$4.08	$4.61	$5.42	$6.79	$9.54
2.875	$3.51	$4.15	$4.68	$5.48	$6.85	$9.60
3.000	$3.58	$4.22	$4.74	$5.55	$6.91	$9.66
3.125	$3.65	$4.28	$4.81	$5.61	$6.97	$9.71
3.250	$3.73	$4.35	$4.87	$5.67	$7.03	$9.77
3.375	$3.80	$4.42	$4.94	$5.74	$7.09	$9.83
3.500	$3.87	$4.49	$5.01	$5.80	$7.15	$9.89
3.625	$3.95	$4.56	$5.07	$5.86	$7.21	$9.95
3.750	$4.03	$4.63	$5.14	$5.93	$7.27	$10.01
3.875	$4.10	$4.70	$5.21	$5.99	$7.33	$10.07
4.000	$4.18	$4.77	$5.28	$6.06	$7.40	$10.12
4.125	$4.26	$4.85	$5.35	$6.13	$7.46	$10.18
4.250	$4.34	$4.92	$5.42	$6.19	$7.52	$10.24
4.375	$4.42	$4.99	$5.49	$6.26	$7.59	$10.30
4.500	$4.50	$5.07	$5.56	$6.33	$7.65	$10.36
4.625	$4.58	$5.14	$5.63	$6.39	$7.71	$10.42
4.750	$4.66	$5.22	$5.70	$6.46	$7.78	$10.48
4.875	$4.74	$5.29	$5.77	$6.53	$7.84	$10.55
5.000	$4.82	$5.37	$5.85	$6.60	$7.91	$10.61
5.125	$4.91	$5.44	$5.92	$6.67	$7.97	$10.67

Rate	40 years	30 years	25 years	20 years	15 years	10 years
5.250	$4.99	$5.52	$5.99	$6.74	$8.04	$10.73
5.375	$5.07	$5.60	$6.07	$6.81	$8.10	$10.79
5.500	$5.16	$5.68	$6.14	$6.88	$8.17	$10.85
5.625	$5.24	$5.76	$6.22	$6.95	$8.24	$10.91
5.750	$5.33	$5.84	$6.29	$7.02	$8.30	$10.98
5.875	$5.42	$5.92	$6.37	$7.09	$8.37	$11.04
6.000	$5.50	$6.00	$6.44	$7.16	$8.44	$11.10
6.125	$5.59	$6.08	$6.52	$7.24	$8.51	$11.16
6.250	$5.68	$6.16	$6.60	$7.31	$8.57	$11.23
6.375	$5.77	$6.24	$6.67	$7.38	$8.64	$11.29
6.500	$5.85	$6.32	$6.75	$7.46	$8.71	$11.35
6.625	$5.94	$6.40	$6.83	$7.53	$8.78	$11.42
6.750	$6.03	$6.49	$6.91	$7.60	$8.85	$11.48
6.875	$6.12	$6.57	$6.99	$7.68	$8.92	$11.55
7.000	$6.21	$6.65	$7.07	$7.75	$8.99	$11.61
7.125	$6.31	$6.74	$7.15	$7.83	$9.06	$11.68
7.250	$6.40	$6.82	$7.23	$7.90	$9.13	$11.74
7.375	$6.49	$6.91	$7.31	$7.98	$9.20	$11.81
7.500	$6.58	$6.99	$7.39	$8.06	$9.27	$11.87
7.625	$6.67	$7.08	$7.47	$8.13	$9.34	$11.94
7.750	$6.77	$7.16	$7.55	$8.21	$9.41	$12.00
7.875	$6.86	$7.25	$7.64	$8.29	$9.48	$12.07
8.000	$6.95	$7.34	$7.72	$8.36	$9.56	$12.13
8.125	$7.05	$7.42	$7.80	$8.44	$9.63	$12.20
8.250	$7.14	$7.51	$7.88	$8.52	$9.70	$12.27
8.375	$7.24	$7.60	$7.97	$8.60	$9.77	$12.33
8.500	$7.33	$7.69	$8.05	$8.68	$9.85	$12.40
8.625	$7.43	$7.78	$8.14	$8.76	$9.92	$12.47
8.750	$7.52	$7.87	$8.22	$8.84	$9.99	$12.53
8.875	$7.62	$7.96	$8.31	$8.92	$10.07	$12.60
9.000	$7.71	$8.05	$8.39	$9.00	$10.14	$12.67
9.125	$7.81	$8.14	$8.48	$9.08	$10.22	$12.74
9.250	$7.91	$8.23	$8.56	$9.16	$10.29	$12.80
9.375	$8.00	$8.32	$8.65	$9.24	$10.37	$12.87
9.500	$8.10	$8.41	$8.74	$9.32	$10.44	$12.94
9.625	$8.20	$8.50	$8.82	$9.40	$10.52	$13.01
9.750	$8.30	$8.59	$8.91	$9.49	$10.59	$13.08
9.875	$8.39	$8.68	$9.00	$9.57	$10.67	$13.15
10.000	$8.49	$8.78	$9.09	$9.65	$10.75	$13.22
10.125	$8.59	$8.87	$9.18	$9.73	$10.82	$13.28
10.250	$8.69	$8.96	$9.26	$9.82	$10.90	$13.35
10.375	$8.79	$9.05	$9.35	$9.90	$10.98	$13.42
10.500	$8.89	$9.15	$9.44	$9.98	$11.05	$13.49
10.625	$8.98	$9.24	$9.53	$10.07	$11.13	$13.56
10.750	$9.08	$9.33	$9.62	$10.15	$11.21	$13.63
10.875	$9.18	$9.43	$9.71	$10.24	$11.29	$13.70
11.000	$9.28	$9.52	$9.80	$10.32	$11.37	$13.78
11.125	$9.38	$9.62	$9.89	$10.41	$11.44	$13.85
11.250	$9.48	$9.71	$9.98	$10.49	$11.52	$13.92
11.375	$9.58	$9.81	$10.07	$10.58	$11.60	$13.99
11.500	$9.68	$9.90	$10.16	$10.66	$11.68	$14.06
11.625	$9.78	$10.00	$10.26	$10.75	$11.76	$14.13
11.750	$9.88	$10.09	$10.35	$10.84	$11.84	$14.20

Rate	40 years	30 years	25 years	20 years	15 years	10 years
11.875	$9.98	$10.19	$10.44	$10.92	$11.92	$14.27
12.000	$10.08	$10.29	$10.53	$11.01	$12.00	$14.35
12.125	$10.19	$10.38	$10.62	$11.10	$12.08	$14.42
12.250	$10.29	$10.48	$10.72	$11.19	$12.16	$14.49
12.375	$10.39	$10.58	$10.81	$11.27	$12.24	$14.56
12.500	$10.49	$10.67	$10.90	$11.36	$12.33	$14.64
12.625	$10.59	$10.77	$11.00	$11.45	$12.41	$14.71
12.750	$10.69	$10.87	$11.09	$11.54	$12.49	$14.78
12.875	$10.79	$10.96	$11.18	$11.63	$12.57	$14.86
13.000	$10.90	$11.06	$11.28	$11.72	$12.65	$14.93
13.125	$11.00	$11.16	$11.37	$11.80	$12.73	$15.00
13.250	$11.10	$11.26	$11.47	$11.89	$12.82	$15.08
13.375	$11.20	$11.36	$11.56	$11.98	$12.90	$15.15
13.500	$11.30	$11.45	$11.66	$12.07	$12.98	$15.23
13.625	$11.40	$11.55	$11.75	$12.16	$13.07	$15.30
13.750	$11.51	$11.65	$11.85	$12.25	$13.15	$15.38
13.875	$11.61	$11.75	$11.94	$12.34	$13.23	$15.45
14.000	$11.71	$11.85	$12.04	$12.44	$13.32	$15.53
14.125	$11.81	$11.95	$12.13	$12.53	$13.40	$15.60
14.250	$11.92	$12.05	$12.23	$12.62	$13.49	$15.68
14.375	$12.02	$12.15	$12.33	$12.71	$13.57	$15.75
14.500	$12.12	$12.25	$12.42	$12.80	$13.66	$15.83
14.625	$12.22	$12.35	$12.52	$12.89	$13.74	$15.90
14.750	$12.33	$12.44	$12.61	$12.98	$13.83	$15.98
14.875	$12.43	$12.54	$12.71	$13.08	$13.91	$16.06
15.000	$12.53	$12.64	$12.81	$13.17	$14.00	$16.13
15.125	$12.64	$12.74	$12.91	$13.26	$14.08	$16.21
15.250	$12.74	$12.84	$13.00	$13.35	$14.17	$16.29
15.375	$12.84	$12.94	$13.10	$13.45	$14.25	$16.36
15.500	$12.94	$13.05	$13.20	$13.54	$14.34	$16.44
15.625	$13.05	$13.15	$13.30	$13.63	$14.43	$16.52
15.750	$13.15	$13.25	$13.39	$13.73	$14.51	$16.60
15.875	$13.25	$13.35	$13.49	$13.82	$14.60	$16.67
16.000	$13.36	$13.45	$13.59	$13.91	$14.69	$16.75
16.125	$13.46	$13.55	$13.69	$14.01	$14.77	$16.83
16.250	$13.56	$13.65	$13.79	$14.10	$14.86	$16.91
16.375	$13.67	$13.75	$13.88	$14.19	$14.95	$16.99
16.500	$13.77	$13.85	$13.98	$14.29	$15.04	$17.06
16.625	$13.87	$13.95	$14.08	$14.38	$15.13	$17.14
16.750	$13.98	$14.05	$14.18	$14.48	$15.21	$17.22
16.875	$14.08	$14.16	$14.28	$14.57	$15.30	$17.30
17.000	$14.18	$14.26	$14.38	$14.67	$15.39	$17.38
17.125	$14.29	$14.36	$14.48	$14.76	$15.48	$17.46
17.250	$14.39	$14.46	$14.58	$14.86	$15.57	$17.54
17.375	$14.49	$14.56	$14.68	$14.95	$15.66	$17.62
17.500	$14.60	$14.66	$14.78	$15.05	$15.75	$17.70
17.625	$14.70	$14.77	$14.87	$15.15	$15.84	$17.78
17.750	$14.80	$14.87	$14.97	$15.24	$15.92	$17.86
17.875	$14.91	$14.97	$15.07	$15.34	$16.01	$17.94
18.000	$15.01	$15.07	$15.17	$15.43	$16.10	$18.02

Glossary

Abstract of title. An abstract of title is used in certain parts of the country in determining if there are any previous claims on the property in question. The abstract is a written record of the historical ownership of the property and helps to determine whether the property can in fact be transferred from one party to another without any previous claims.

Acceleration. A loan accelerates when it's paid off early, usually at the request or demand of the lender. This is usually associated with an acceleration clause within a loan document that states the circumstances under which a loan must be paid immediately, but most usually applies when payments are late or missed or when transfer of the property takes place without the lender's permission.

Adjustable-rate mortgage. A loan program where the interest rate may change over the life of the loan. The rate is adjusted in accordance with agreed-upon terms between the lender and the borrower, but typically changes only once or twice a year.

Amortization. The process of paying off a loan fully over a period time through equal payments made at regular intervals. The length of time over which the loan is repaid is stipulated in a predetermined agreement. Such a loan is sometimes called a fully amortized loan. Amortization terms can vary, but generally accepted terms run in 5-year increments from 10 to 40 years.

Annual Percentage Rate (APR). The APR is the cost of money borrowed, expressed as an annual rate. It is a useful consumer tool for comparing different lenders, but unfortunately it often is not used correctly. The

APR works for comparisons only when the same exact loan type from one lender to another is being compared. It doesn't work as well when comparing different types of mortgage programs with different down payments, terms, and so on.

Appraisal. A report used in determining the market value of a property. This report can be done in various degrees of detail as required by a lender, from simply driving by the property in a car to making a full-blown inspection complete with full-color photographs of the real estate. Appraisals compare similar homes in the area that would substantiate the value of the property in question.

Assumable mortgage. A mortgage that allows buyers to take over the terms of the loan along with the house being sold. Assumable loans may be fully or nonqualifying assumable, meaning that buyers can take over the loan without being qualified or otherwise evaluated by the original lender. With qualifying assumable loans, while buyers may assume the terms of the existing note, they must qualify as if they were applying for a brand-new loan.

Automated valuation model. An electronic method of evaluating a property's appraised value based upon scanning public records for recent home sales and other data in the subject property's neighborhood. This is not yet widely accepted as a replacement for a full-blown appraisal, but many people expect AVMs to eventually replace traditional appraisals altogether.

Balloon mortgage. A type of mortgage where the remaining balance must be paid in full at the end of a preset term. A five-year balloon mortgage might be amortized over a thirty-year period but have the remaining balance be due, in full, at the end of five years.

Banker. A lender who uses its own funds. Historically these funds would have come from the savings accounts of other bank customers. But with the evolution of mortgage banking, that's the old way of doing business. Even though bankers use their own money, that money may come from other sources, such as lines of credit, or from selling loans to other institutions.

Basis point. 1/100 percent. 25 basis points is $^{1}/_{4}$ of a discount point. 100 basis points is 1 discount point.

Bridge loan. A short-term loan primarily used to pull equity out of one property to make a down payment on another. This loan is paid off when the original property is sold. Since these are short-term loans, sometimes just for a few weeks, usually only retail banks will offer them. Usually the borrower doesn't make any monthly payments and pays off the entire loan when the property is sold.

Brokers. Mortgage companies that set up a home loan for a borrower with a banker, similar to the way an independent insurance agent operates. Brokers don't have money to lend directly but have experience in finding various loan programs that can suit the borrower. Brokers don't work for the borrower, but instead provide mortgage loan choices from other mortgage lenders.

Bundling. The act of putting together several real estate or mortgage services in one package. Instead of paying for an appraisal here and an inspection there, some or all of the services the buyer needs are packaged together. Usually this is to offer discounts on all services, although when services are bundled it's hard to see whether you're getting a good deal or not.

Buying down. Paying more money to get a lower interest rate. This is called a permanent buydown, and it is used in conjunction with discount points. The more points, the lower the rate. A temporary buydown is a fixed-rate mortgage where the rate is reduced for the first period, then gradually increases to its final rate. A temporary buydown for two years is called a 2-1 buydown. A buydown for three years is called a 3-2-1 buydown.

Cashing out. Taking equity out of a home in the form of cash during a refinancing. Instead of just reducing your interest rate during a refinancing and financing your closing costs, you finance even more, putting the money in your pocket.

Closing costs. The various fees involved in buying a home or obtaining a mortgage. The fees can be charged directly by the lender or in the transactions that are required in order to issue a good loan.

Collateral. Property owned by the borrower that's pledged to the lender to be returned in case the loan goes bad. A lender makes a mortgage with the house as collateral.

Comparable sales. The part of an appraisal report that lists recent transfers of similar properties in the immediate area of the house being bought. Also called "comps."

Conforming loan. A conventional loan that is equal to or less than the maximum allowable loan limits established by Fannie Mae and Freddie Mac. These limits are changed annually.

Conventional loan. A mortgage that is made using guidelines established by Fannie Mae or Freddie Mac and is issued and guaranteed by lenders.

Credit report. A report showing a consumer's payment history along with the consumer's property addresses and any public records.

Debt consolidation. Paying off all or part of one's consumer debt with equity from a home. This can be part of a refinanced mortgage or a separate equity loan.

Debt ratio. Gross monthly payments divided by gross monthly income, expressed as a percentage. There are typically two debt ratios to be considered: The housing ratio, sometimes called the front ratio, is the total monthly house payment plus any monthly tax, insurance, PMI, or homeowners' association dues divided by gross monthly income, and the total debt ratio, also called the back ratio, is the total housing payment plus other monthly consumer installment or revolving debt, also expressed as a percentage. Loan debt ratio guidelines are usually denoted as 32/38, with 32 being the front ratio and 38 being the back ratio. Ratio guidelines can vary from loan to loan and from lender to lender.

Deed. A written document evidencing each transfer of ownership in a property.

Deed of trust. A written document giving an interest in the home being bought to a third party, usually the lender, as security for the loan.

Delinquent. Being behind on a payment. Delinquencies typically are recognized as 30 + days delinquent, 60 + days delinquent, and 90 + days delinquent.

Discount points. A percentage of a loan amount; 1 point equals 1 percent of the loan balance. Borrowers pay discount points to reduce the interest rate on a mortgage, typically by $^1/_4$ percent for each discount point paid. It is a form of prepaid interest to a lender. Also called "points."

Document stamp. Evidence of a tax paid—usually with a literal ink stamp—upon transfer of ownership of property. Document stamp tax rates can vary based upon locale. Some states don't have document stamps. Also called "doc stamp."

Down payment. The amount of money initially given by the borrower to close a mortgage, equal to the sales price less financing. It's the very first bit of equity you'll have in the home.

Easement. A right of way previously established by a third party. Easement types can vary but typically involve such things as the right of a public utility to cross your land to access an electrical line.

Equity. The difference between the appraised value of a home and any outstanding loans recorded against the house.

Escrow. This can mean two things, depending upon where you live. On the West Coast, there are escrow agents whose job it is to oversee the closing of a home loan. In other parts of the country, an escrow is a financial account set up by a lender to collect the money for annual tax bills and/or hazard insurance policy renewals in monthly installments.

Escrow agent. On the West Coast, the person or company that handles the home closing, ensuring that documents are assigned correctly and the property has legitimately changed hands.

Fed. Typically used to refer to the Federal Reserve Board. The Fed, among other things, sets overnight lending rates for banking institutions. It doesn't set mortgage rates.

Federal Home Loan Mortgage Corporation (FHLMC or Freddie Mac). A corporation established by the U.S. government in 1968 to buy mortgages, made under Freddie Mac guidelines, from lenders.

Federal Housing Agency (FHA). An agency formed in 1934 and now a division of the Department of Housing and Urban Development (HUD). It provides loan guarantees to lenders who make loans under FHA guidelines.

Federal National Mortgage Association (FNMA or Fannie Mae). A corporation originally established in 1938 by the U.S. government to buy FHA mortgages and provide liquidity in the mortgage marketplace. Its function is similar to that of Freddie Mac. In 1968 its charter was changed, and now it purchases conventional mortgages as well as government ones.

Fee income. Closing costs received by a lender or broker other than interest or discount points. Fee income can take the form of loan processing charges, underwriting fees, and the like.

Final inspection. The last inspection of a property, showing that a new home being built is 100 percent complete or that a home improvement is 100 percent complete. This lets the lender know that its collateral and its loan are exactly where they should be.

Fixed-rate mortgage. A mortgage where the interest rate does not change over the term of the loan.

Float down. A mortgage loan rate that can drop as mortgage rates drop. There are two types of float, with one being used during the construction of a home and the other being used during the period of an interest-rate lock.

Floating. Actively deciding not to "lock" or guarantee an interest rate while a loan is being processed. This is usually done because the borrower believes that rates will go down.

Foreclosure. The bad thing that happens when the mortgage isn't repaid. Lenders begin the process of forcibly recovering their collateral when borrowers fail to make loan payments. The lender takes your house away.

Fully indexed rate. The number reached when a loan's index and the margin are added. This is the rate used for adjustable-rate notes.

Funding. The actual transfer of money from a lender to a borrower.

Gift. When buying a home, funds used for the down payment and closing costs that are given to the borrower(s) instead of coming from their own accounts. Usually such gifts can come only from family members or from foundations established to help new homeowners.

Good faith estimate. A list of estimated closing costs on a particular mortgage transaction. This estimate must be provided to the loan applicants within 72 hours after receipt of a mortgage application by the lender or broker.

Government National Mortgage Association (GNMA or Ginnie Mae). A corporation formed by the U.S. government to purchase government loans like VA and FHA loans from banks and mortgage lenders. Think of it as Fannie Mae or Freddie Mac, except that it buys only government loans.

Hazard insurance. A type of insurance that covers against certain destructive elements, such as fire, wind, and hail. It's usually an addition to homeowner's insurance, but every home loan has a hazard rider.

Home equity line of credit (HELOC). A credit line using a home as collateral. The customer writes a check on the line whenever he needs it and pays only on balances withdrawn. It's much like a credit card that is secured by property.

Homeowner's insurance. An insurance policy covering not just hazard items but also other things such as liability or personal property.

Impound accounts. Accounts set up by a lender in which monthly payments of annual property taxes or hazard insurance are deposited. As the taxes come due or the insurance comes up for renewal, the lender pays the bill using these funds. Also called "escrow accounts."

Index. The figure used as the basis for calculating an interest rate, usually with a margin added to it. Almost anything can be an index, but the most common are the rates on U.S. Treasuries or similar instruments. See Fully indexed rate.

Inspection. A structural review of the house that looks for defects in workmanship, damage to the property, or lack of required maintenance. It does not determine the value of the property. A pest inspection looks for things such as termites, wood ants, and so on.

Intangible tax. A state tax collected on personal property. An intangible asset is an asset not in itself but through what it represents. A publicly traded stock is an intangible asset. It's not the stock itself that has the value, but what the stock represents in terms of income and ownership.

Interest rate. The amount charged to borrow money over a specified period of time.

Jumbo loan. A mortgage that exceeds current conforming loan limits.

Junior lien. A second mortgage or one that is subordinate to another loan. This term is not as common as it used to be. You're likely to hear simply "second mortgage" or "piggyback."

Land contract. An arrangement in which the buyer makes monthly payments to the seller, but the ownership of the property does not change hands until the loan is paid in full. This is similar to the way an automobile loan works. When you finish paying for the car, you get the title.

Land to value. An appraisal term that calculates the value of the land as a percentage of the total value of the home. If the value of the land exceeds the value of the home, it's more difficult to find financing without good comparable sales. Also called "lot to value."

Lender policy. Title insurance that protects a mortgage lender from defects in title or previous claims of ownership.

Liability. An obligation. Liabilities can be those that show up on a credit report, such as student loans or a car payment, but they can also be anything else that one is obligated to pay. They are the obligations on the credit report that are used to determine debt ratios.

Loan. Money given to one party by another with the expectation of its being repaid.

Loan officer. The person typically responsible for helping mortgage applicants get qualified, who assists in loan selection and loan application. Loan officers can work at banks, credit unions, or mortgage brokerage houses or for bankers.

Loan processor. The person who gathers the required documentation on a loan application for submission. Along with your loan officer, you'll work with this person quite a bit during your mortgage process.

Lock. The act of guaranteeing an interest rate over a predetermined period of time. Loan locks are not loan approvals; they're simply the rate your lender has agreed to give you at loan closing.

Margin. A number, expressed as a percentage, that is added to a mortgage's index to determine the rate the borrower pays on the note. If the index is a six-month CD at 4.00 percent and the index is 2.00 percent, the interest rate that the borrower pays is $4 + 2$, or 6.00 percent. The fully indexed rate is the index plus the margin.

Market value. In an open market, the value of a property that is both the highest that the borrower was willing to pay and the lowest that the seller was willing to accept at the time of contract. Property appraisals help justify market value by comparing the prices at which similar homes in the subject property's neighborhood were sold.

Mortgage. A loan on property with the property being pledged as collateral. The mortgage is retired when the loan is paid in full.

Mortgage-backed securities. Investment securities issued by Wall Street firms that are guaranteed, or collateralized, with home mortgages taken out by consumers. These securities can then be bought and sold on Wall Street.

Mortgage Insurance (MI). An insurance policy, paid by the borrower with benefits paid to the lender, that covers the difference between the borrower's down payment and 20 percent of the sales price. If the borrower defaults on the mortgage, this difference is paid to the lender. Mortgage insurance, also called private mortgage insurance (PMI), is typically required on all mortgage loans with less than 20 percent down.

Mortgagee. The person or business making the loan.

Mortgagor. The person(s) getting the loan; the borrower(s).

Multiple listing service (MLS). A central repository where real estate brokers and agents show homes and search for homes that are for sale.

Negative amortization (neg am). An adjustable-rate mortgage that has two interest rates, the contract rate and the fully indexed rate. The contract rate is the minimum agreed-upon rate that the consumer may pay; sometimes the contract rate is lower than the fully indexed rate. The borrower has a choice of which rate to pay, but if the contract rate is lower than the fully indexed rate, that difference in payments is added to the loan. If your payment at the contract rate is only $500 but the payment at the fully indexed rate is $700 and you pay only the contract rate, $200 is added to your original loan amount. These mortgages are not for the faint of heart or for those with little money down.

Nonconforming. A mortgage loan amount that is above current Fannie Mae or Freddie Mac limits. Also called a "jumbo" mortgage.

Note. A promise to repay. There may or may not be property involved, and it may or may not be a mortgage.

Origination fee. A fee charged to cover costs associated with finding, documenting, and preparing a mortgage application, usually expressed as a percentage of the loan amount.

Owner's policy. Title insurance that protects the homeowner.

Points. See discount points.

Prepaid interest. Daily interest collected from the day of the loan closing to the first of the following month.

Prepayment penalty. A monetary penalty paid to the lender if the loan is paid off before its maturity or if extra payments are made on the loan. Penalties are sometimes divided into "hard" and "soft" penalties, where a hard penalty is one that is automatic if the loan is paid off early or extra payments are made at any time or for any amount whatsoever. A soft penalty lasts for only a couple of years and may allow extra payments on the loan, not to exceed a certain amount.

Principal. The outstanding amount owed on a loan, not including any interest due.

Principal, interest, taxes, and insurance (PITI). The figures used to determine front debt ratios.

Private mortgage insurance. See mortgage insurance.

Realtor. A member of the National Association of Realtors. This is a registered trademark, and not all real estate agents are Realtors.

Refinancing. Obtaining a new mortgage to replace an existing one.

Sales contract. A written agreement, signed by both the seller and the buyer, to buy or sell a home.

Second mortgage. A mortgage that assumes a subordinate position behind a first mortgage. If the home goes into foreclosure, the first mortgage would be settled in full before the second could lay claim. Sometimes called a "piggyback" mortgage.

Secondary market. A financial arena where mortgages are bought and sold, either individually or grouped together into securities backed by those mortgages. Fannie Mae and Freddie Mac are the backbone for the conventional secondary market. Other secondary markets exist for nonconforming loans, subprime loans, and other types.

Seller. The person transferring ownership and all rights in a home in exchange for cash or other assets.

Settlement statement. A document that shows all financial entries during the home sale, including sales price, closing costs, loan amounts, and property taxes. Your initial good faith estimate will be your first glimpse of your settlement statement. This statement is one of the final documents put together before you go to closing and is prepared by your attorney or settlement agent. Also called the "final HUD-1."

Survey. A map that shows the physical location of the structure and where it sits on the property. It also designates any easements that run across or through the property.

Title. Ownership in a property.

Title exam/title search. The process in which public records are reviewed to discover any previous liens on the property.

Title insurance. An insurance policy that protects the lender, the seller, and/or the borrower against any defects in title or previous claims to the property being transferred or sold.

Index

Look for These Exciting Real Estate Titles at
www.amacombooks.org/realestate

A Survival Guide for Buying a Home by Sid Davis $17.95

A Survival Guide for Selling a Home by Sid Davis $15.00

Are You Dumb Enough to Be Rich? by G. William Barnett II $18.95

Everything You Need to Know Before Buying a Co-op, Condo, or Townhouse by Ken Roth $18.95

Make Millions Selling Real Estate by Jim Remley $18.95

Mortgages 101 by David Reed $16.95

Real Estate Investing Made Simple by M. Anthony Carr $17.95

The Complete Guide to Investing in Foreclosures by Steve Berges $17.95

The Consultative Real Estate Agent by Kelle Sparta $17.95

The Home Buyer's Question and Answer Book by Bridget McCrea $16.95

The Landlord's Financial Tool Kit by Michael C. Thomsett $18.95

The Property Management Tool Kit by Mike Beirne $19.95

The Real Estate Agent's Business Planner by Bridget McCrea $19.95

The Real Estate Agent's Field Guide by Bridget McCrea $19.95

The Real Estate Investor's Pocket Calculator by Michael C. Thomsett $17.95

The Successful Landlord by Ken Roth $19.95

Who Says You Can't Buy a Home! by David Reed $17.95

Your Successful Real Estate Career, Fourth Edition, by Kenneth W. Edwards $18.95